GUIDES TO MATERIALS FOR
WEST AFRICAN HISTORY IN EUROPEAN ARCHIVES

4

FRANCE

GUIDES TO MATERIALS FOR WEST AFRICAN
HISTORY IN EUROPEAN ARCHIVES

MATERIALS FOR WEST AFRICAN HISTORY IN FRENCH ARCHIVES

by

PATRICIA CARSON

UNIVERSITY OF LONDON
THE ATHLONE PRESS
1968

Published by
THE ATHLONE PRESS
UNIVERSITY OF LONDON
at 2 *Gower Street, London* WC1
Distributed by Constable & Co Ltd
12 *Orange Street, London* WC2

Canada
Oxford University Press
Toronto

U.S.A.
Oxford University Press Inc
New York

© *University of London,* 1968

485 17204 6

Printed in Great Britain by
WESTERN PRINTING SERVICES LTD
BRISTOL

CONTENTS

Part II. Archives and Libraries Outside Paris

CONTENTS   vii

INTRODUCTION

THE purpose of this *Guide* is to indicate the manuscript material relating to the history of West Africa, between Saint-Louis in the north and the Congo river in the south, to be found in the archives and libraries of France. This material consists of the records of individual traders and groups of traders, including chambers of commerce, together with the archives of the government departments concerned with the French West African territories. The records of the earliest contacts with West Africa are chiefly to be found in the archives of the northern French seaboard towns, such as Honfleur, Saint-Malo and Le Havre, where organized companies trading to those parts first arose. To these there succeeded during the great period of the slave trade, which came later, the archives of Nantes, Bordeaux and La Rochelle. The relevant archives of the central government in Paris, becoming increasingly important from the early eighteenth century onwards, are, down to 1894, those of the Ministry of the Marine, and after that date those of the Colonial Office. These may be supplemented by material to be found in the archives of the Ministry of Foreign Affairs, although the great bulk of the records of that office relate to the diplomatic struggle for the partition of Africa, an aspect of African history which, in accordance with the general plan of this series of *Guides*, has been omitted. Records of the period before 1789 are preserved in the Archives Nationales. After that date they are in principle to be sought in general at the relevant Ministry. The records of the local administrations in the French colonies, of which copies were not sent to Paris, remain in the central government archives of Afrique occidentale française (AOF) in Dakar, or in one of the various African territorial archives. There is a splendid collection of maps in the Bibliothèque Nationale. In addition to these collections of private and official papers, both central and provincial, there are missionary archives which contain valuable information. They are, however, difficult of access, except for those deposited in the Vatican, which have been dealt with in the *Guide to materials for West African history in Italian Archives*. But an important group of documents in the archives of the Fathers of the Holy Spirit in Paris is noted here.

THE ARCHIVE SYSTEM IN FRANCE

France is covered by a network of centralized national or departmental archives, and by a decentralized system of municipal archives. The central governmental archives are preserved for the period before 1789 almost entirely in the Archives Nationales. After that date succeeding deposits of archive material have been made by various ministries and the dates which limit these vary from one ministry to another. Where material is not held by the Archives Nationales it may be found in the Ministry of Foreign Affairs, the Ministry of Marine, or the Ministry of Colonies. The various departmental archives depend on the central administration but contain the regional archives. The more important towns have their own communal archives, and sometimes possess family and commercial papers from the region.

LIBRARIES AND MUSEUMS

There is a network of public libraries in France, of which the Bibliothèque Nationale is the centre; and these contain important manuscript collections. By far the greatest quantity of relevant material is preserved in the Bibliothèque Nationale. But there is also much to be found in the municipal libraries. There are valuable collections in the libraries, although the latter are not rich in West African material.

ACCESSIBILITY

Departmental and communal archives are open to the public although sometimes, particularly in the smaller towns, it is wise to write in advance. Permission to work in the Archives Nationales must be applied for in advance and some of the material which is deposited there may only be consulted after obtaining a special authorization from the Ministry concerned or ultimately from the Ministry of Foreign Affairs. Students are advised to use great care in obtaining the necessary authorizations. Missionary archives are strictly private, although special authorizations are sometimes granted. Permission is also needed for work in the archives of the Chambers of Commerce.

A permit is necessary for admission to the Bibliothèque Nationale and an additional card of admission for the manuscript department.

BIBLIOGRAPHICAL AIDS

There is a list of national, departmental and communal archives in *Archivum*, V, 1955. Ch. V. Langlois and H. Stein, *Les archives de l'histoire de France* (Paris, 1891), published as vol. I in the series *Manuels de bibliographie historique*, provides a general introduction to French archive material. The two volumes *Archives nationales: Etat sommaire par série des documents conservés aux archives nationales*, Paris, 1891, and *Etat général par fonds des archives départementales*, Paris, 1903, form an indispensable general synopsis. Innumerable inventories are listed in *Etat des inventaires des archives nationales, départementales, communales et hospitalières au 1er janvier 1937*, by H. Courteault, Paris, 1938, continued in the *Supplément, 1937–1954*, by R. H. Bautier, Paris, 1955. For information about current archival work see R. H. Bautier, *Bibliographie analytique internationale des publications relatives à l'archivistique et aux archives*, published in *Archivum*, II, 1952.

An invaluable list of library catalogues is contained in *Latin Manuscript Books before 1600*, by P. O. Kristeller, 3rd ed., New York, 1965. There is a short guide, *Bibliothèques de France, Description de leurs fonds et historique de leur formation*, by C. Serrurier, The Hague, 1946, and a survey of *Les catalogues imprimés de la Bibliothèque Nationale*, Paris, 1953. The two main catalogues for French public libraries, excluding the Bibliothèque Nationale are the *Catalogue général des manuscrits des bibliothèques publiques des départements*, 7 vols. in-4°, Paris, 1849–85, and *Catalogue général des manuscrits des bibliothèques publiques de France, Départements*, Paris, 1886 *et seq.* (51 vols. in-8° to date). A most important volume of the *Bibliographie générale des colonies françaises* is devoted to West Africa: *Bibliographie de l'Afrique occidentale française*, by E. Joucla, Paris, 1937.

PART I

ARCHIVES AND LIBRARIES IN PARIS

National Archives

Archives Nationales, 60 rue des Francs-Bourgeois, Paris IIIe

The French national archives are open to the public on the presentation of a diplomatic or university letter of introduction. The reading room is open from Monday to Saturday from 10 a.m. to 6 p.m., although documents cannot be obtained between 11.30 a.m. and 1 p.m. or after 5 p.m. It is possible to obtain microfilms of many documents. There is a *Guide du Lecteur* in the reading room. Material in the national archives falls into two main chronological sections: the period before 1789, *Section ancienne*, and that after 1789, *Section moderne*. Within each of these sections there are subdivisions designated by letters. In addition to the general collection many documents have been deposited by particular ministries: notably by the Ministries of Foreign Affairs, Marine, and Overseas Territories.[1] Information concerning West Africa must be sought chiefly in the documents of either Overseas Territories or of the Marine, of which the former was an offshoot.

Both sections of the Archives of the Marine and of the Colonies which are deposited in the Archives Nationales, i.e. *Archives anciennes* and *Archives modernes*, are classified in the *Section ancienne*. In the following lists, the series of documents appear in the order in which they are found in the *Etat des inventaires des Archives nationales, départementales, communales et hospitalières au 1er Janvier 1937* (see below).

Of the general inventories and repertories the most important are: *Inventaire sommaire et tableau méthodique des fonds conservés aux Archives nationales* (1st part: documents before 1789), Paris, 1871; and *Etat sommaire par séries des documents conservés aux Archives nationales*, Paris, 1891. These two inventories complement each other, the first being a more general view of the documents conserved in the national archives and of the series into which they are divided, while the second provides more precise information about the documents and more exact references. Another equally important guide is the *Etat des inventaires des Archives nationales, départementales, communales et hospitalières au 1er Janvier 1937*, and its *Supplément*, which brings the list down to 31 July 1955. Many of the inventories and repertories listed in these works are available in the reading room; others must be specially requested.

[1] Some records deposited by the *Service historique de la Marine* and by the *Section Outre-Mer* have different chronological divisions. See appropriate sections.

I. Section Ancienne

Series K. Historical Monuments (*Monuments historiques*)

1232. The end of the description by de la Courbe of his visit to the African　　　1
Coast, 1685.[1]

Series N and NN. Plans and maps

Répertoire numérique des plans, 3 registers, 2 boxes of cards (Inventory 252).
Volume IV. Seine-et-Marne, Zuiderzee, colonies and foreign countries, including:

SENEGAL

F 50–22, M 1023. R. Gambia and fort of St. James, eighteenth century　　　2

N III 2. Map of the island of Goree, n.d.　　　3

N II 1. Map of the R. Niger from its mouth to the island of St. Louis, and a　　　4
view of the fort, n.d.

N III 5. Plan of Portendic, n.d.　　　5

N III 4. Plan of the fort of St. Louis, n.d.　　　6

N III 1. Map of the colony of Senegal, n.d.　　　7

N III 3. Map of the mouth of R. Senegal, n.d.　　　8

Series Z 1-D. Juridictions spéciales et ordinaires: Amirauté de France[2]

Répertoire numérique, by E. Berger.
Z^1-D 71. Papers of various companies concerned in the slave trade etc.,　　　9
1767.

Z^1-D 72. The same, 1767.　　　10

Z^1-D 102 A. The same, 1767.　　　11

Z^1-D 102 B. The same, 1768.　　　12

Old Colonial Office

(*Ancien bureau des consulats: Affaires étrangères, BI, BIII.*)

These documents consist of two series: B I, *Correspondance consulaire*, to which
there is a guide, *Répertoire numérique de la sous-série B I*, by L. Celier (MS.
inventory 929); and B III, *Répertoire numérique de la sous-série B III*, by L. Celier
(MS. inventory 929 bis).

The *Series B* I contains consular documents from the Ministry of Foreign
Affairs for the period before 1793, which are divided between this series and
Marine B 7. There may be documents concerning West Africa in, for example,
the consular correspondence with Amsterdam: no 165, 1775–84.

---

[1] Published by P. Cultru as *Premier voyage du Sieur de la Courbe fait à la Coste d'Afrique
en 1685*, Paris, 1913. For the earlier part of this manuscript see section below on the
Bibliothèque Nationale, mss. fr. 24221 and 24222.
[2] See introductory note on archives of the Ministry of Marine, p. 32.

Series B III. Papiers de l'ancien Bureau des Consulats
Contains various reports and memoranda:

COLONIAL ARCHIVES
(*Archives des Colonies*)

These documents consist of those deposited in the National Archives in 1910 when the modern series, for the period after 1790, were left in the Ministry, rue Oudinot.[1] For the history of West Africa the most fruitful series are Series B (correspondence despatched) and Series C (correspondence received), of which many of the originals are retained in the Marine Series. Other information may be sought in Series F (commercial companies, missions, etc.). There is a general guide, *Répertoire numérique*, by P. de Vaissière, completed by Y. Bezard, J. Mallou and P. Daudet, 1928–35 (MS. inventory 527, 983); a *Table alphabétique des dossiers du personnel des Colonies jusqu'en 1789 (Série E)*, by P. de Vaissière (12 boxes of cards, inventory 972), a *Table alphabétique du personnel colonial, 1790–1860*, by M.-L. Boulard and T. Tour (in course of compilation); and a *Table alphabétique générale du personnel colonial, 1860–1948*, by M.-L. Boulard and T. Tour (70,000 entries, kept up to date). In the colonial archives in the rue Oudinot there is a card index for Series B and C. A. Mirot, *Catalogue des documents concernant les missions catholiques conservés aux Archives nationales*, may also be consulted.

Series B. Letters despatched
Some are boxes of documents, others bound as registers.

---

[1] For further details of the series in this section see the remarks on the archives of the Ministry of Marine, p. 32, and of the Ministry of French Overseas Territories, p. 65.

Series C. Correspondence received

C 6. Sénégal ancien.[1]

---

[1] There is no inventory of this series but it has been very extensively used by A. Delcourt, *La France et les établissements français au Sénégal entre 1713 et 1763*, Dakar, 1952. The documents are classed chronologically.

[1] Published by H. Froidevaux in *La découverte de la chute du Félou*, Paris, 1899.

[1] This document has been extensively used by H. Labouret and P. Rivet in *Le Royaume d'Arda et son évangélisation au XVIIe siècle. Travaux et mémoires de l'Institut d'Ethnologie*, VII, Paris, 1929.

[1] Published in full by A. Delcourt, *op. cit.*, p. 10 above.

[1] Printed in full by A. Delcourt, *op. cit.*, p. 10 above.

[1] Printed in full by A. Delcourt, *op. cit.*, p. 10 above.

---

[1] Printed in full by A. Delcourt, *op. cit.*, p. 10 above.

[1] All the other documents in C 6. 13 relate to Anamabou (Guinea).

Report on Senegal, 1 June 1762.   **594**

Questionnaire on Senegal, 30 October 1762.   **595**

Report on possibility of recapturing Senegal, n.d.   **596**

15. General correspondence of Goree and dependencies, 1763–8.   **597**
    E.g., Report by M. Adanson on the island of Goree and French
Guyane.[1] Description of an expedition made by Aussenac on R. Falémé,
1758–9, and a report on the state of the garrison and provisions, 1763.
Report on the gum trade, 1762. Report on the slave trade, 1762. Report
by Governor Desmesnagers on the Albréda post, and the desirability of
exchanging territory with England, 1765. Report by Morel, on trade
possibilities of the rivers Saloum and Gambia, 1771.[2] Reports by Doumet
on Goree, 1773.

16. General correspondence of Goree and dependencies, 1768–75.   **598**
    E.g., Instructions for the governor Maretz de Montchaton and Bone-
face (Goree).[3] Report on Portuguese encroachments during the Seven
Years' War at Bissao, 1775. Note on the new African company, 1773.
Reports by Governor Le Brasseur.[4] Report on the poor prospects for
Goree by Governor de Rocheblave.

17. Includes: **599**
    E.g., Report on the administration of Senegal, 1777. Report by de
Capelles, captain of the *Epervier*, on the resources of the rivers of Senegal,
1779. Reports by Lauzun and Pontevez-Gien on the abandonment of
Goree and removal to St. Louis, 1779, 1780. Reports on the slave trade,
n.d.

18. Instructions of Governor Dumontet, 1782.[5]   **600**

Report on the slave trade.   **601**

Report by Lé Brasseur on bad conditions in Goree, 1783.   **602**

Instructions of Governor de Repentigny, 1783.[6]   **603**

The same for de Boufflers, 1784.[6]   **604**

Letter from de Beauvoir about the kingdom of Ouaire, and extracts from   **605**
the report by Oliver Montaguerre, director of Whydah, on trade there,
1787.[7]

---

[1] Edited by H. Froidevaux in *Les Mémoires inédits d'Adanson sur l'île de Gorée et a
Guyane française*, Paris, 1899.
[2] Partly published by J. Machat in *Documents sur les établissements de l'Afrique occidentale
au XVIIIe siècle*, Paris, 1906.
[3] Both printed in full by C. Schefer in *Instructions générales données de 1763 à 1870 aux
gouverneurs et ordonnateurs des établissements français en Afrique occidentale*, 2 vols., Paris,
1921.
[4] Many papers of Le Brasseur were brought together by Le Brasseur himself and are in
the Bibliothèque Nationale, MS français 12080.
[5] Published by C. Schefer, *op. cit.*
[6] Text in C. Schefer, *op. cit.*
[7] Published by P. Roussier, 'Documents sur les relations entre la France et le royaume de
Ouaire à la Côte d'Afrique (1784–1787)' in *Bulletin du Comité d'Etudes historiques et
scientifiques de l'AOF*, vol. XI, Paris, 1928.

[1] See Gaillard, 'La terrible vengeance du capitaine Landolphe' in *Bulletin . . . de l'AOF*, vol. IX, Paris, 1926.
[2] Published by C. Schefer, *op. cit.*, p. 28 above.

27, 27 bis. Includes: **630**
> E.g., undated reports of the period before 1790. Information about the kingdom of Benin, 1785; Senegal, 1779–1801; Amokou, 1802. Copy of treaty of Dubourdieu for establishing a fort at Anamabou, 1752. Report on the end of the French possession of Whydah, 1804. Report on its population, n.d. Plan of the village of Gregoy and road to quay of St. Louis (Whydah), 1776. Plan of fort of Whydah, 1776. Plan to improve it, 1777. Description of the different forts of all nations on the Guinea coast, 1795.[1]

28. Includes:
> E.g., documents concerning *inter alia* Kommenda and relations with   **631** the Dutch, 1667–90. Taccorary, 1687. Isigny, 1692–1702. Reports and maps by Abbé Bullet, before 1785. Reports on two missionaries sent to Goree, Father Chevalier and Father Chapelet, 1775–8.

29. Includes, e.g., Map of the mouth of R. Senegal and island of St. Louis,   **632** n.d. Report on the Arguin affair, n.d. Reports on Senegal before 1814.

30. Includes, e.g., Letters exchanged by the French and English trading   **633** companies, n.d. Various reports and plans, 1683–1802.

Series D. Colonial Troops

See *Répertoire numérique,* by P. de Vaissière etc., cited on p. 9 above.

D 2C. Lists and inspections of colonial troops

[1] Published by S. Berbain in *Le comptoir français de Juda (Ouidah) au XVIIIe siècle, Etude sur la traite des noirs au golfe de Guinée,* Paris, 1942. The author makes extensive use of the documents in C 6, 25, 26, 27, and 27bis, which are classified chronologically.

Series F. Commercial companies, missions, etc.

fo. 67–73. Plan for consolidating the colony of Senegal, 1779.
fo. 74–78. Memorandum on the need to conquer the island of Goree, 1782.
fo. 82–97. Papers about the purchase of arms, 1783.
fo. 98–122. Quarrels about expenses, 1783.
fo. 136. Report on Senegal, 1784.
fo. 143–149. Report concerning the Goree garrison, 1784.
fo. 152–63. Reports on negotiations with other colonies, quarrels with King Damel, re-establishment of the post at Joal, 1784.

61. Documents concerning Africa, 1727–89. **666**

62. Same, Senegal, n.d. **667**

128. Same, slave trade, 1788–90. **668**

129. Same, *An* VII. **669**

F 5B. Travellers
Many documents concerning passengers to the colonies.

33. Register concerning, *inter alia*, Senegal, 1820–30. **670**

Series J. Posts vacant

1, 6. Posts vacant in *inter alia*, Senegal, 1819–51. **671**

12, 369–80. Dossiers concerning civilian and military personnel deceased **672** in, *inter alia*, Senegal, 1836–60.

Series K. Papers concerning the compensation of the owners of slaves etc., after 1848

8. Senegal. **673**

MARINE ARCHIVES
(*Archives de la marine*[1])

(a) Archives anciennes[2]

The *Etat sommaire des archives de la marine antérieures à la révolution*, by Didier Neuville, Paris, 1898, provides a general view of this archive. Of the Series A, which consists of acts, ordinances, edicts etc., *Actes du pouvoir souverain*, there are several eighteenth- and nineteenth-century inventories, but it is not very

[1] Before the creation of a separate ministry of Colonies in 1894, the Ministry of Marine was responsible for the French Territories overseas, through its colonial office. Documents concerning the colonies were often conserved in duplicate, the original in the Ministry of Marine itself and a copy in this colonial office. All documents from this office from the period before 1789 were later deposited in the National Archives, as were all documents from the Ministry of Marine for the period before 1870. This series of the Marine therefore consists of documents of which some duplicates may be found in the documents of the Colonial Archives deposited in the National Archives for documents for the period before 1789, and in the archives of the Ministry of Overseas Territories for documents for the period between 1789 and 1870.
[2] See introductory note, p. 7.

likely that material interesting for West Africa will be found there. The Series B, which includes general correspondence, decisions, orders, and despatches (*Service général*), will be found much more fruitful. It has been inventoried by D. Neuville and H. Buche: *Inventaire des Archives de la Marine, Série B: service général*, 7 vols., Paris, 1885–1913, and two MS. vols., the nine volumes divided as follows: I: B 1 1–102, B 2 1–75; II: B 2 76–243; III: B 2 244–435; IV: B 3 1–119; V: B 3 120–233; VI: B 3 234–379; VII: B 3 380–560; VIII in MS. only: B 3 560–797; IX in MS. only (Supplement, 1664–1789): B 3 789–803. There is also a card index: *Table alphabétique des volumes 4 à 9 de l'inventaire imprimé et manuscrit de la série B3 (Correspondance reçue)*, by M.-L. Boulard, B. Bouriello and T. Tour (inventory 116 consisting of sixteen boxes of cards). For the Series B 1 (decisions of the *Conseil de la Marine* 1686–1789), a detailed inventory of the first thirty-seven numbers (1654–1715) has been made by E. Taillemite.

Series B 1

1. fo. 70. Complaints about interlopers by the Compagnie de Sénégal, and Bruë's report on the condition of the Company, 1715. **674**

4. fo. 192, 322. Information about the natives on the Guinea coast, 1716. **675**

5. fo. 342–50. Request from the Compagnie de Sénégal for the confiscation of an English ship, the *Elisabeth*, Captain Marmaduke Payne, because he had been buying slaves from King Amel. Extensive description of the slave trade on this coast, 1716. **676**

8. fo. 18, 563, 567. Report on the trade of Guinea, 1716. **677**

9. fo. 500. Report on Bruë in Senegal, 1716. **678**

19. fo. 1. Report on the trading post of Whydah and merchandise suitable for the country, 1717. **679**

fo. 200. Accounts of the director of the above, 1717. **680**

20. fo. 134. Complaint about the bad quality of slaves from Benin, 1717. **681**

27. fo. 118, 119. Report on the affairs of the Compagnie de Sénégal, 1718. **682**

28. fo. 33, 71, 79, 131, 149, 164, 179, 192, 200, 216, 313, 316, 464. Reports on the fort of Whydah, 1718. **683**

fo. 466, 467. Report on the trade of Senegal, 1718. **684**

40. fo. 30. Complaint that the Portuguese were attempting to take over Cape Three Points, 1719. **685**

43. fo. 8. Ships destined for Senegal, 1719. **686**

60. fo. 126. Description of the *Griffon*'s voyage to the coast of Senegal, prompted by English attempts to invade the gum trade of Portendic, 1738. **687**

80. fo. 152. Mention of a voyage to the same coast by the *Etourdie*, 1774. **688**

87. On the behaviour of the duke of Lauzun after the conquest of Senegal, 1778. **689**

90. Complaint by a merchant from Bordeaux about difficulties experienced by him in his slaving depot in Senegal, 1779. **690**

[1] Most of the registers of correspondence in this series are prefaced by tables of contents.

Series B 4. Campagnes. 1572–1789

This section contains correspondence, reports, accounts, descriptions of expeditions etc. The classification is usually geographical and chronological.

7. Description of the capture of Goree by d'Estrées, 1677.   771

12. The squadron's reports from the Guinea Coast, 1689–90.   772

21. Report on the slave trade, 1701.   773

23. Description of the capture and ransom of the fort of Gambia taken   774
from the log of the *Mutine* and the *Hermine*, containing details of the
country, clothes, natives, chiefs in the countryside round the R. Gambia
and the island of Goree, and a description of d'Amon's voyage and the
foundation and establishment of Isigny, 1700.

25. 1703.   775

26. 1704, 1705.   776

29. 1705, 1706.   777

31. 1706.   778

34. 1709, 1710.   779

36. 1711–15.   780

38. 1721–5 (e.g., Log of the *Griffon* and the *Vénus*, with a description of   781
Arguin and its king, the slave trade, the local language, mariguette
pepper, the many forts on the Gold Coast, Whydah, St. Thomas' island,
1721. Letter from the captain of the *Apollon* in Port Louis with an
abridged account of the voyage along the coast, 1723).

45. Senegal, 1738–9.   782

49. Same, 1746.   783

63. Descriptions of disputes between the English and French, 1749–51.   784

65. Report by Périer de Salvert from the Guinea coast, 1752.   785

66. Description of a battle off the West African coast, 1753.   786

103. Reports from Guinea, 1760–2.   787

115. Observations on the West African coast, n.d.   788

125. Particulars of the supplies necessary for the slave trade in Cape Verde,   789
1775.

149. Plan for an expedition to the Guinea coast, and Senegal and the   790
destruction of the English trading posts on the R. Gambia, and details
about the military activities of de Chevigny on the R. Senegal, 1779.

196. Details about the conquest of Senegal, and the attack on the island of   791
Goree, and destruction of the English establishments in Sierra-Leone,
1781.

214. Plan for an expedition to West Africa, 1774–80.   792

267. Description of an expedition by the *Vénus* in Angola and Cabinda,   793
1783, 1784.

270. Report on the establishment of the fort on the island of Gambia, 1785.   794

274. Details of the slave trade, 1787.   **795**

280. Expedition of *Néréide* to Guinea and a description of the merchant   **796**
ships there, 1789.

Series C. Personal archives

Many naval personnel have separate dossiers which contain chiefly information
concerning their salaries, professional positions etc. but in some cases there are
additional details, although it is essential to know the name of the person concerned in order to discover relevant matter. There is a list *Table alphabétique des
dossiers du personnel de la Marine, dont les services sont antérieurs à 1789 (sous-série C 7)*
by Le Cacheux, R. André-Michal and Y. Bézard (7 boxes of cards, inventory 525).
The continuation is to be found in the Series CC (*Archives modernes*). (E.g., *C 7
196*: dossier of *de Marillac*, commander of the *Amazone* off the West African coast,
especially at Portendic with de Bruë, 1717.)

(b) Archives modernes[1]

Series AA 1-3

This series of ordinances, decrees, and regulations (*actes du pouvoir exécutif*)
remained in the archives of the Marine even after the Ministry of Colonies was
formed in 1894, but such documents as referred to West Africa were placed in
the Series BB 4.

Series BB. Service général

There is a guide to this series: *Répertoire numérique des séries BB 1 à BB 8, avec une
introduction et table alphabétique*, by Paul Marichal, 1900 (MS. inventory 692).
This covers documents of the period before 1870. Part of this series appears in the
*Inventaire analytique de BB 1 1–133 (rapports du ministre au chef de l'Etat et rapports
au ministre, décisions de 1789 à 1864) de BB 2 cl–477, 546–8, 772–86 (correspondance
ministérielle, lettres envoyées, de 1790 à 1869)* by Georges Bourgin, 1913, which was
brought up to date later (MS. inventory 693).

For the Series BB 3, which contains correspondence received, there is a manuscript inventory: *Inventaire analytique de BB 3 1–849, 1124–44* (nos. 850–1123
having not been deposited in the national archives) by G. Bourgin (MS. inventory
693). It contains, however, only the names of those from whom letters have been
received, but nothing about their contents.

Series BB 4. Campagnes

Inventaire analytique BB 4 1–1052 (Campagnes de 1790 à 1869), by G. Bourgin,
1913 (MS. Inventory 693)[2] and the *Supplément, comprenant BB 4 1752–1832
(Campagnes de 1794 à 1872)*, by G. Bourgin, 1920–21 (MS. inventory 935) and
the *Table alphabétique des deux inventaires précédents de la sous-série BB 4* by G.
Bourgin, 1921–3 (eight boxes of cards; inventory 945).

445. Includes reports from ships off the coast of Senegal, 1823.   **797**

449. Papers of the *Béarnaise*, on a voyage to Senegal, 1823.   **798**

[1] See introductory note, p. 7.
[2] The first part of this inventory B 4 1–320 (1790–1811) has been published in the
Revue Maritime, vols. CXCV–CXCVII, Oct. 1912 to Dec. 1914.

456. Includes reports from the West African station, 1824.   **799**

460. Includes reports from the *Chameau*, the *Lyonnais* and the *Vénus*, off   **800**
Senegal, 1824.

471. Includes circular to the commanders of squadrons and naval stations   **801**
about the slave trade, and the case of the captain of the *Hippolyte*, con-
demned for taking part in the trade, 1826.

474. Includes reports on the movement of shipping in Goree habour, 1826.   **802**

484. Includes log-books of ships off the Senegal coast, 1826, 1827.   **803**

485. Includes notes on the *Flore*, including hydrographical information and   **804**
correspondence, 1826, 1827.

488. Includes papers about the sinking of the *Juliette* in the harbour of St.   **805**
Louis, 1828.

489, 504, 516, 520, 539. Include reports from the West African coast,   **806**
1827–30.

534bis. Secret correspondence and reports from Senegal, 1830.   **807**

541. Report on the voyage of the *Railleuse* to the coast of Senegal, 1831.   **808**

555, 563. Same from the *Assas* from Senegal, the *Flore*, and the *Seine*, 1833.   **809**

556. Report on a military expedition to the Walo country.   **810**

Extensive memorandum from the captain of the *Cigogne* on relations   **811**
with the English in Sierra Leone.

Report on activities against Spanish and Portuguese slave traders.   **812**

Particulars of a native prince of Benin travelling with the French, 1833.   **813**

562. Report from West African fleet, 1834.   **814**

569. Same, from the *Abondance* from Senegal, Guyane, and the Antilles,   **815**
1835.

575. Same, from the African naval station and from the *Dordogne* and the   **816**
Recherche from Senegal, 1836.

577, 580. Same, 1837.   **817**

582. Reports from the *Girafe*, the *Loire*, and the *Recherche* from Senegal.   **818**

586, 588, 594. Reports from the West African naval squadron, 1838, 1839.   **819**

595. Report from the *Triomphante* from West Africa, 1839.   **820**

602. Reports from captains etc. on difficulties with the English.   **821**

Treaties with native chiefs, their presents (embroidered uniforms),   **822**
medals to be given to natives helping the French, 1840.

610. Reports from the *Didon*, the *Fine*, the *Tarn* from West Africa, 1841.   **823**

614, 615. Reports from the West African squadron, and the *Africaine* from   **824**
Senegal, 1842.

621. Same, from the *Alcmène, Africaine, Egérie, Eperlan*, 1843.   **825**

627, 633, 635. Reports from the West African squadron, 1844, 1845.   **826**

636. Report from the *Héliopolis*, 1845.   **827**

Series GG. Mémoires et documents divers

There is a typed inventory of this series: *Inventaire sommaire de GG 1 1–198*
(mémoires et projets de 1786 à 1884), no. 987.[1]

Carton 45.

Series JJ. Service hydrographique
Series 4 JJ. Log-books, seventeenth-nineteenth centuries

Inventaire analytique de la sous-série 4 JJ (journaux de bord, XVIIe-XIXe siècle) avec
table alphabétique divisée en deux parties (1⁰ journaux de bord antérieurs à 1800; 2°
journaux de bord postérieurs à 1800), by Georges Bourgin (MS. inventory 940).

[1] This inventory has been put together with those for the Series GG 2 and GG 3.

		Ship	Captain	Home Port	Destination	Date	
27	2	Duc de Noailles	Siccard	Lorient	Senegal, Martinique, St. Domingue	1722	867
	3	Mutine	de la Rigaudière	do	do	do	868
	4	Maréchal d'Estrées	Landouine	do	do	do	869
	5	Jason	de Marguaissac	do	do	1723	870
	6	Vénus	Gaulthier	do	do	do	871
	7	Dauphin	Filouze	do	do	do	872
	8	Maure	Cazaneau	do	do	1724	873
	9	Galathée	Brithelair	do	do	1725	874
	10	Dryade	Lefevre	do	Goree	do	875
		Aurore	Siccard	do	Senegal, American islands	do	876
	11	Marie	de Tourneville	do	Senegal, St. Domingue	do	877
28	20	Néréide	d'Antaly	do	Senegal, Martinique, St. Domingue	1729	878
	23	Duc de Bourbon	de Broisy	do	do	1730	879
	25	Baleine	Vaubercy	do	do	1731	880
	29	Alexandre	Chouquet	do	do	1732	881
	32	Gironde	de Prudhomme		do	1733	882
	35	Saint-Louis	Bienvenu	Lorient	Senegal, Martinique, St. Domingue	1734	883
	36	Aigle	de Kerandran	do	do	do	884
29	45–6	Aigle	Solain-Baron	do	Senegal	1736	885
	49	Comtesse	Rocher Sorin	do	Senegal, Martinique	1737	886
	52	Henriette	Marguerin	do	Senegal, Martinique, St. Domingue	1739	887
	53	Flore	Lachaise	do	do	do	888
30	65	Valeur	Libordière	do	do	1740	889
	66	Comtesse	Le Houx	do	do	do	890
	67	Aurore	Haumont	do	do	do	891
	68	Marie	Bigost de la Canté	do	do	do	892
	69	Apollon	Tibodière	do	Senegal	1740, 43	893
	70	Flore	Lachaise	do	do	1740	894
	71	Saint-Michel	—	do	do	1741	895
	72	Favorite	de Sanguinet	do	do	1743	896
	74	Comtesse	Le Houx	do	Senegal, Martinique	1746	897
	76	do	do	do	do	do	898
31	76	Duc de Chartres	de Sanguinet	do	Senegal, Martinique, St. Domingue	1746	899
	77	Duc de Chartres	de Sanguinet	Lorient	Senegal, Martinique, St. Domingue	1747	900
34	2	Arc-en-Ciel	d'Amblimont	Rochefort	St. Laurent, Goree, Martinique	1687	901

		Ship	Captain	Home Port	Destination	Date	
61	7	Vénus	de Cou-lombe	Brest	Lagos	1737	902
	13	Flore	de Crenay	Toulon	West African coast	do	903
	22	Various ships	—	—	Cape Verde	1759	904
62	1–8	Various ships	—	—	Senegal	1723–53	905
	9	Espérance	Horry	—	do	1723	906
	10	do	—	Lorient	do	do	907
	11	do	—	—	do	do	908
	12	Apollon	de la Rigau-dière	—	do	do	909
	13	Eléphant	Pichon	—	do	1724	910
	14	Duc du Maine	Périer de Salvert	—	do	do	911
	15	Astrée	Bataille	—	Goree, Senegal and Gambia	1727	912
	16	Deux Frères	Pichon	—	Senegal	1725	913
	17	Gironde	Pichon	—	do	1726	914
	18	Astrée	Genino	—	do	1726	915
	19	do	Bataille	—	do	1727	916
	20	Léopard	Pigeon	—	do	do	917
	21	do	do	—	do	do	918
	22	Volage	Copaux	—	do	1728	919
	23	Espérance	d'Antaly	Lorient	Senegal	1728	920
	24	Duc d'Orléans	Penmance	—	do	do	921
	25	Vénus	do	—	do	do	922
	26	do	do	—	do	do	923
63	27	Flore	Penmance	—	Senegal and Goree	do	924
	28	do	do	—	do	do	925
	29	Volage	—	—	—	do	926
	30	Espérance	d'Antaly	—	Senegal	do	927
	31	Duc d'Orléans	—	—	do	do	928
	32	Vénus	La Renau-dais	—	do	1729	929
	33	Amiral	Kerguenelle	Lorient	do	do	930
	34	Duc d'Orléans	Pommier	—	Portendic	do	931
	35	do	do	—	do	do	932
	36	Néréide	d'Antaly	—	Cape Blanc, Porten-dic, Senegal and Louisiana	do	933
	37	Fier Cavalier	Duel-Chouquet	Lorient	Senegal and Goree	1730	934
	38	Astrée	Baston	—	Senegal	1730	935
	39	Saint-Michel	de Trédillac	Lorient	Senegal and Goree	do	936
	40	do	do	do	do	do	937
64	41	Fier Cavalier	Duel-Chouquet	—	do	do	938
		—	de Trédillac	—	West African coast	1732	939

	Ship	Captain	Home Port	Destination	Date	
42	Fier Cavalier	Duel-Chouquet	—	Senegal	1730	940
43	Astrée	Barton	—	Senegal, Goree	do	941
44	Courrier d'Orléans	Smidt	Lorient	Senegal	do	942
45	Américain	Aubin Duplessis	—	do	1731	943
46	Baleine	Vaubercy	—	do	do	944
47	do	do	—	do	do	945
48	Annibal	Lobry	—	do	do	946
49	Alexandre	Chouquet	Lorient	do	1732	947
50	Néréide	Boisquenay	do	do	do	948
51	do	do	do	do	do	949
52	Courrier d'Orléans	Arniol	Bordeaux	Senegal, Goree	do	950
53	do	do	do	do	do	951
54	Fier Cav.	Castelnaux	Lorient	Senegal, Gambia	do	952
55	Saint-Michel	Lobry	—	Senegal, Portendic	do	953
56	Fier Cav.	Castelnaux	Lorient	Senegal, Goree, Gambia	do	954
57	Courrier d'Orléans	Amiot	—	Senegal	1733	955
58	do	de Zoufreville	—	do	1732	956
59	Saint-Michel	Lobry	—	do	1733	957
60	Gironde	Prud-homme	Lorient	Senegal, St. Domingue	do	958
61	Aigle	Kaudran	do	Senegal, Martinique	1734	959
62	Aurore	Solain-Baron	Lorient	Senegal, Goree, Gambia	1735	960
63	Aigle	do	do	do	1736	961
64	do	do	do	Senegal, Goree, St. Domingue	do	962
64bis	do	—	do	Senegal, American islands	1737	963
65	Saint-Louis	Bienvenu	do	Senegal, Goree, St. Domingue	1735	964
66	Aurore	Solain-Baron	—	Senegal	1736	965
67	Gloire	de la Marre	Lorient	Senegal, Azores	do	966
68	do	do	do	do	do	967
69	Fleuron	Gencien	Brest	Goree	1737	968
70	do	do	do	do	do	969
71	do	do	do	Portendic, Goree	do	970
72	Badine	Lachaise	Lorient	Senegal	do	971
73	Saint-Michel	Bocquet	—	do	1737–8	972
74	Griffon	Périer	Brest	Canaries, Portendic	1738	973
75	do	do	do	do	do	974
76	Astrée	do	do	Cape Blanc, Cadiz	do	975
77	Courrier d'Orléans	de Calloès	—	Senegal	1740	976
78	Prudente	—	—	do	1739	977

		Ship	Captain	Home Port	Destination	Date	
	79–80	Gloire	Bocquet	—	Senegal	1739	**978**
	81	Comtesse	—	—	do	1741	**979**
	82	Saint-Michel	La Salle du Bournay	—	do	1740	**980**
	83	Gloire	Maugruin	—	do	1741	**981**
66	84	Prince de Conti	Sanguinet	—	do	do	**982**
	85	Henriette	du Clos	—	Senegal	1741	**983**
	86–7	Fière	Behourd	—	do	do	**984**
	88	Aurore	Haumont	—	do	do	**985**
	89	Henriette	Lozier-Bouvet	—	do	1742	**986**
	90	Apollon	de la Tibodière	—	do	1743	**987**
	91	Maurepas	Sanguinet	—	do	do	**988**
	92	Cygne	Beaumont	—	do	1749	**989**
	93	Chevalier Marin	d'Après	Lorient	do	do	**990**
	94	do	do	do	do	do	**991**
	95	Zéphyr	Bonsoleil	—	do	do	**992**
	96–8	Paon	Blanchet Duvergé	—	do	do	**993**
	99	Valeur	Chasseur	—	do	1750	**994**
	100	Cybèle	Cagnons	—	do	do	**995**
	101	Sainte-Reine	d'Estre	—	do	1753	**996**
	102	Hirondelle	—	—	do	do	**997**
	103	Cybèle	Cagnons	—	do	do	**998**
	104	Renommé	Brumonier	—	do	do	**999**
	105	Légère	Motte-Gaillard	—	do	1756	**1000**
	105bis	do	do	—	do	do	**1001**
67	106	Saint-Luc	Montet	—	do	1759	**1002**
	107	Duc d'Orléans	Berger	Lorient	do	1731–2	**1003**
	108	do	do	do	do	do	**1004**
	109	César	Le Large	I. d'Aix	Goree island	1765	**1005**
	110	Bergère	Villeneuve	Rochefort	Goree	1767	**1006**
	111	Gorée	Le Large	do	Canaries, Goree	do	**1007**
	113	Rossignol	Brach	do	Senegal, Gambia	1785	**1008**
	114	Cérès	Dangely de Payolle	Brest	Goree, Cape Rouge, Gambia	1786	**1009**
	115	do	do	do	From Gambia and Brest	1787	**1010**
	116	Outarde	Sablières	Rochefort	Cape Verde, Senegal etc.	do	**1011**
69	2	Saemslag	La Chapelle	Brest	Guinea, American islands	1704	**1012**
	4	Galathée and Cupidon	Parant	Nantes	Guinea etc.	1710	**1013**
	5	extract from 4.				do	**1014**
	6	Vénus	Courserac	Brest	Guinea	1721	**1015**

		Ship	Captain	Home Port	Destination	Date	
	7	extract from 6				1721	**1016**
	9	*Annibal*	Hardouin	Nantes	Guinea, American islands	1723	**1017**
	10	do	do	do	Guinea	do	**1018**
	11	*Jupiter*	Monnier	Lorient	Guinea, American islands	do	**1019**
	12	*Junon*	Crasson	—	do	do	**1020**
	13	do	do	—	do	do	**1021**
	14	*Duc de Bourbon*	Tessier	Bordeaux	do	1724	**1022**
	15	*Africain*	Lalande-Boulaux	Lorient	do	do	**1023**
	16	*Méduse*	Hermitte	—	do	1725	**1024**
	17	*Dryade*	de Sève	—	do	do	**1025**
	18	*Flore*	de la Marre	—	do	do	**1026**
	19	*Languedocien*	Légier	Havre	do	1726	**1027**
	20	*Languedocien*	Légier	Havre	Guinea, American islands	1726	**1028**
70	21	*Duc de Noailles*	Dupuis	Lorient	Guinea coast, American islands	1727	**1029**
	22	do					
	23	*Pontchartrain*	Rocher-Sorin	—	do	do	**1030**
	24	do					
	25	*Dromadaire*	de la Marre	Lorient	Guinea, American islands	1733	**1031**
	26	do					
	27	*Flore*	de la Tibodière	do	do	1734	**1032**
	28	*Badine*	Bart	do	do	1735	**1033**
	29	*Vestale*	Boisquenay	do	do	1737	**1034**
	30	*Henriette*	de la Marre	do	do	1738	**1035**
	31	*Vestale*	do	do	do	1740	**1036**
71	32	*Favorite*	Prudhomme	do	do	do	**1037**
	33	*Flore*	Zouffreville	do	do	1741	**1038**
	34	*Comtesse*	Castellan	do	do	1742	**1039**
	35	*Flore*	Colombier	Havre	do	do	**1040**
	36	do	do	do	do	do	**1041**
	37	*Vestale*	Le Houx	Lorient	do	1743	**1042**
	38	*Argonaute*	de la Londe	—	Cape of Good Hope, Coast of Angola	1747	**1043**
	39	*Triton*	du Tertre	Lorient,	Guinea, American islands	1749	**1044**
	40	*Content*	Glandèves	Toulon	Guinea, Gibraltar	1750	**1045**
	41	*Oriflamme*	Nouvet	do	do	do	**1046**
	41bis	*Anémone*	Sané	Brest	Guinea, American islands	1751	**1047**
	42	*Protée*	Montlouet	do	Guinea	1753	**1048**
	43	do	do	do	do	do	**1049**
	44	extract from no. 42				do	**1050**
	47	*Reine*	Mamineau	do	From Loanda to Lorient	1754	**1051**

		Ship	Captain	Home Port	Destination	Date	
	49	Dauphin	—	—	Loanda	1755	**1052**
	50	—	de Cau-mont	Brest	Guinea, Angola, American islands	1756	**1053**
	51	Calypso	Caro	—	Guinea	1765	**1054**
	51bis	Aimable Henriette	La Cou-draye	Havre	do	—	**1055**
		Duguay-Trouin	do	Mar-seilles	do	—	
		Babillarde	—	—	Angola	1773–6	**1056**
	52	Roi de Congo	do	Ostend	Guinea and Angola	1783	**1057**
	53	Dorade	Dubois	Rochefort	Senegal, Guinea	1774	**1058**
	54	Afrique Mouche	Dessaux-Monta-gaud	do	Goree, Guinea, American islands	1775 do	**1059**
	54bis	do	do	—	do	do	**1060**
	55	Castries	de Gouyon	—	Cape of Good Hope, Cape Volta	1776	**1061**
72	57	Blonde	Tour du Pin	Toulon	Gambia, Bissage	1784	**1062**
	59	Dordogne	Villemagne	Brest	Senegal, Guinea	1786	**1063**
	60	Junon	de Flotte	do	Guinea	do	**1064**
73	61	Flore	Bonna-venture	Rochefort	Senegal, Guinea	1787	**1065**
	62	Cousine	Martin	do	do	do	**1066**
	63	Fauvette	de la Baume	do	do	do	**1067**
	64	Eveillé	de Boube	do	do	1788	**1068**
	66	Favori	Lincoll	—	Angola	1738	**1069**
325	—	Infatigable	—	—	Senegal, West Africa, Brazil	⎰ 1815–16 / 1819 / 1822–3 ⎱	**1070**
326	—	Loire	Gicquel des Touches	—	Senegal, West Africa	1816, 1820	**1071**
327	1	Bayonnaise	Allègre	—	Senegal	1817–22	**1072**
	2	Prudente	—	—	Senegal, West Africa	1818–19	**1073**
328	—	Isère	—	—	do	⎰ 1819–22 / 1823 ⎱	**1074**
329	—	Charente	—	—	Senegal, Antilles	1818–20	**1075**
330 331	—	Huron	du Plessix	—	Senegal, West Africa	1820–2	**1076**
332	1	Nantaise	Lemaigre	—	do	1820–3	**1077**
	2	Ménagère	Taillard	—	do	1820–1	**1078**
333	—	Cauchoise	Missiessy	—	do	⎰ 1820–22 / 1826 ⎱	**1079**
334	1	Argus	Meslay	—	Galam expedition	1818–20	**1080**
	2	Bressanne	Maudet	—	—	1823–5	**1081**
	3	Salamandre	—	—	Senegal (troopship)	1824–5	**1082**
335	—	Dragon	Lachelier	—	Senegal, West Africa	1823–6	**1083**
337	—	Momus	de Gauts	—	Senegal, West Africa	⎰ 1823–4 / 1824–5 ⎱	**1084**
338	—	Marsouin	Danyean	—	Spain, West Africa	1823–5	**1085**
339	1	Bressanne	Maudet	—	Senegal, West Africa	1825–7	**1086**
	2	Meuse	Genebrias	—	Senegal, Brazil	1826	**1087**

		Ship	Captain	Home Port	Destination	Date	
340		*Lilloise*	Leprédour	—	Hydrography of West African coast	1831–3	**1088**
341	*1*	*Champenoise*	Deguise	—	Senegal, West African coast	1829–34	**1089**
	2	*Bordelaise*	Duvaure	—	do	1829–32	**1090**
342	*1*	*Assas*	Pujol	—	do	1831–2	**1091**
	2	*Dunois*	—	—	do	1833–4	**1092**
	3	*Hermione*	Brou	—	do	1831–2	**1093**
344		*Nisus*	de la Rogue	—	do	{ 1838–40 1841–4	**1094**
345		*Malouine*	Bouët	—	do	1837–44	**1095**
346		*Pénélope*	Bouët-Wil-laumez	—	do	1849–50	**1096**
411		*Caraibe*	do	—	Senegal (sunk)	1845–7	**1097**
412		*Eldorado*	Maissin	—	Senegal, West African coast	1847–9	**1098**

Series 5 JJ. 'Petites archives', log-books, eighteenth and nineteenth century

Inventaire analytique de la sous-série 5 JJ, avec table alphabétique, by G. Bourgin (MS. inventory 941).

HYDROGRAPHY

4d. Report on the west coast of Africa, n.d.   **1099**

205. Villemain papers: notes on, and views of Liberia, Gold Coast, Ivory   **1100** Coast, Gulf of Benin, Calabar, Gabon, Gulf of Biafra, Loango, Congo, Angola, Senegal, Senegambia, Sierra Leone, Grain Coast, 1825–52.

207. Two logs of the *Belle Poule* on the West African coast, 1842–3.   **1101**

     Activities of the *Malouine* off the same coast, 1841–4.   **1102**

210. Observations on the R. Gabon, 1847.   **1103**

211. Reports of various voyages, *inter alia*, of the *Alouette* and the *Prudence*,   **1104** containing especially navigational information and materials for a map of R. Nuñez, 1842–7.

216. Report on the expedition of the *Bayadère* to the West African coast,   **1105** 1817–18.

     Maps of the West African coast, 1817.   **1106**

252. Report on the expedition to the West African coast, 1817.   **1107**

255. Observations by Lt. Aymes on Ogonoué, Fernand Paz, Elira N'Coni,   **1108** 1867–8.

256. Annotated copy of the *Manuel de la navigation à la côte occidentale*   **1109** *d'Afrique*, by C. M. Philippes de Kerhallet, 1857–71.

257. Reports on Gabon, with plans of the harbour of Libreville, 1868–9.   **1110**

264. Report on an expedition to Senegal, 1885.   **1111**

260. Report on the voyage of the *Vénus* in the bay of Goree and Dakar, **1112**
1868–9.

Series 6 JJ. Maps. Sixteenth to nineteenth century

Inventaire analytique de la sous-série 6 JJ (cartes, XVIe–XIXe siècles), by G. Bourgin
(MS. inventory 942).

22. Voyages of the *Phare* off the Spanish and African coasts, 1854–5.   **1113**

  II: Portulan of the West African coast of, *inter alia*, St. Louis, Goree, **1114**
  Assini, Grand Bassam, mouth of Bonny river, gulf of Biafra, Gabon,
  n.d.

25. Various maps, *inter alia*, of Sierra Leone, n.d.

35bis. Guinea coast, from Sierra Leone to Cape Lopez, 1750.   **1115**

  West African coast, from Cape Bojador to Sierra Leone, 1753.   **1116**

  Guinea coast from Cape Verga to Cape Lopez, by D'Anville, 1755.   **1117**

  West African coast from Cape Verga to Cape Formosa, by Norrio, **1118**
  1785–97.

  West African coast from Lisbon to Sierra Leone, by K. Moore, 1793.   **1119**

  West African coast from Senegal to Cape St. Anne, by Woodrill, 1794.   **1120**

  West African coast from England to Cape Palmas, by Horsburgh, 1814.   **1121**

  West African coast from Sierra Leone to Cape Formosa, by Van Keulen, **1122**
  n.d.

  West African coast from Sierra Leone to Cape Mogador, by Van Keulen, **1123**
  n.d.

  West African coast from Cape Spartel to Cape Bojador, by de Borda, **1124**
  1780.

  West African coast from Cape Spartel to Cape Bojador, by Van Keulen, **1125**
  1794.

  West African coast from Cape Bojador to Cape Verde, by Van Keulen, **1126**
  1794.

  West African coast from Cape Bojador to Cape Blanc, by Vidal, 1821–9.   **1127**

  West African coast from Cape Spartel to Aganior, by Arlett, 1835.   **1128**

  View of villages on the R. Joal, n.d.   **1129**

  West African coast from Ste. Croix to Cape Bojador, by Arlett, 1835.   **1130**

  Mouths of the rivers Gambia and Galam, MS. n.d.   **1131**

  West African coast from Cape Blanc to the Gambia, after Fleurion, 1739.   **1132**

  West African coast from Cape Blanc to Cape Verga, by D'Anville, 1751.   **1133**

  West African coast from Cape Blanc to the Gambia, by Mannevillette, **1134**
  1781.

  West African coast from Cape Blanc to the Gambia, by Mannevillette, **1135**
  1794.

  Course of the Gambia river, by Owen, 1826.   **1136**

II. Section Moderne

Series F 12. Commerce and industry

The *Etat sommaire des versements faits aux Archives nationales par les ministères et les administrations qui en dépendent*, vol. II, containing the series F 10 to F 17, and a *Table alphabétique des noms de matières, de lieux, de personnes* of the series F 12, dossiers 1 to 2474 B and registers 1 to 383, are to be found in the reading room of the *Section moderne*.

Report on the dangers of navigation.

Question of steamship service to link Sierra Leone, France and Brazil (via Goree), n.d.

Report on French and English commerce on West African coast, Sierra Leone and the Gambia.

Long report on commerce, navigation, politics, geography and statistics of Sierra Leone (translation of report made by Spanish consul there). 1867.

Report on conditions of navigation of Pepel river, n.d.

Report on trade of Lagos, 1882.

Report on commerce of Porto Seguro and the Popos, 1882.

Rates of duties etc. in Sierra Leone, 1882.

Report on Sherbro, 1883.

List of French residents in Sierra Leone, 1896.

4. Sierra Leone, 1858–95.   **1191**

5. Whydah, 1866–95.   **1192**

7208. Reports of various expeditions, and consular commercial correspon- **1193** dence, from Grand Bassam, Liberia, Sierra Leone, 1837–50.

E.g., p. 44, Campaign on the West African coast, by Bouët-Willau-mez, printed, 1850.

Sketch of the commerce of the West African coast.

p. 51, Report on Gallinas to Gabon, by Bouët, printed, 1843.

p. 80, As above from Gallinas to Gabon, by M. Broquant, 1838–9.

Report on Dahomey, 1852.

Report on Liberia, 1856.

Report on Gabon, 1848.

Report on the rivers of Bonny and New Calabar, 1856.

Report on Gold Coast, 1856.

Report on Portuguese posts in West Africa, 1858.

Report on the Gambia, 1853.

p. 109, Report on the exploration of the South, the Gambia and the Rio Pongo, 1837.

Reports on Cape Verde, Senegambia, Côte Malaguette, Sierra Leone, Ivory Coast, Gabon, Gold Coast, Slave Coast, n.d.

Various printed pamphlets and extracts from newspapers.

Various papers about commercial activities of Régis frères of Marseille on West African coast.

Salt and palm oil trade in Rio Nuñez area, 1845.

Documents about the voyage of the *Malouine*, n.d.

Report on capture of Chief Manuel Cringer, 1840.

Information about Whydah, 1850.

Grand Bassam, 1846.

Assini, 1844.

7208, continued.   **1194**

E.g., Report on island of Lagos, 1861.

Extract from newspaper.

Exploration by steamer *Le Gu et-N'Dar* up one of the tributaries of the Assini river.

Investigation of resources of Grand Bassam, 1850, 1851, 1887.

7211. Reports on, *inter alia*, Senegal, 1851–86. **1195**

7212. Report on, *inter alia*, Captain Magnan's exploration as far as the **1196** Niger, 1862–8.

Series AP. Private archives
Series AQ. Economic archives

These documents were previously all grouped in the Series AB. Subsequently they have been divided between various series. They are listed in *Des états sommaires des documents entrés aux Archives nationales par des voies extraordinaires* which appear from time to time in the series *Bibliothèque de l'Ecole des Chartes: Depuis les origines jusqu'a 1917* by Ch.-V. Langlois, vol. lxxviii, 1917, and separately, Paris, 1917; *De 1918 à 1928* by H. Courteault, vol. xc, 1929, and separately, Paris, 1929; *De 1928 à 1941* by G. Bourgin, vol. ciii, 1942, and separately, Paris, 1943; *De 1942 à 1952*, by M. François, vol. cx, 1952, and separately, Paris, 1953, and include:

47 AP. Papers of the explorer H. Duveyrier and his friend, C. Maunoir, **1197** Secretary of the Société de géographie, *inter alia*, in Senegal, 1857–88 (previously *AB XIX 469–78*). Typed inventory.

66 AP. Monteil papers: correspondence and diaries etc. of the Monteil **1198** expedition to Haut-Oubangi and Baoulé, and the Berlin conference on the Cameroons, 1885–1910.

8 AQ. Archives of the third Compagnie des Indes, chiefly administrative, **1199** 1785–91, 1866 (previously *AJ¹*). Inventory by P. Marichal[1] and A. de St. Leger (MS. inventory 885).

AD VII. Collection Rodonneau

This is a collection of printed documents referring chiefly to acts by the central government. It can be used to supplement manuscript material or to fill lacunae.

The *Tableau méthodique des fonds* (1871), cols. 745–846, provides a detailed inventory for the part of this collection of the period before 1789. From 1789 onwards there is a *Répertoire numérique* by de Curzon.

1. Colonies (e.g., Instructions, privileges etc., concerning the East and **1200** West Indies, the Guinea Coast etc., 1665–1789).

3. Slave trade (e.g., Copies of the privileges of the Compagnie de Guinée, **1201** documents about the marriage of slaves, etc., 1670–1789).

Manuscript Collection of the National Archives.[2]

Catalogue des manuscrits conservés aux Archives nationales, Paris, 1892, and *Partie complémentaire du précédent catalogue* (MS. card index).

736 (K 907, no. 39). Memorandum on the trade of Senegal. Eighteenth **1202** century.

917 (K 1232, no. 5 and no. 7). Reports on expedition in West Africa and the **1203** campaign of d'Estrées, 1687 (fragmentary).

---

[1] These documents have been listed by J. Conan in *La dernière Compagnie française des Indes (1785–1875)*, Paris, 1942, using the old code numbers.
[2] These manuscripts are conserved in the Archives Nationales, but do not form part of any of the archive collections.

2741 (T 1393). Report on West African plantations, eighteenth century. **1204**

2766 (T 1527). Instructions from the King for the Duke of Lauzun on how **1205**
to get rid of the English between Cape Blanc and the Sierra Leone river.

Account of Senegal, by de Pontevez, with quite a lot about the natives **1206**
round the French fort St. Louis, 1779 (two copies).

2767 (T 1527). Description of the capture and destruction of Forts James **1207**
and Saccondée, by de Pontevez, n.d.

2768 (T 1527). Report on English possessions and trade in Africa, eighteenth **1208**
century.

Army Archives

Service historique de l'Etat-major de l'armée, Château de Vincennes, Seine

The military archives can be consulted upon a written application to the appropriate ambassador. The reading room is open from 10 a.m. to midday and from 2 to 6 p.m., but an appointment should be made. The *correspondance ancienne* may be consulted, for which see: *Inventaire sommaire des Archives historiques (Archives anciennes (période antérieure à 1792)—correspondance)*, Paris, 1898–1930, 7 vols., with an alphabetical table of subjects in vol. VII and a supplement dealing with *Mémoires historiques, reconnaissances, mémoires techniques*, for which see *Catalogue général des manuscrits des bibliothèques publiques de France, Archives de la guerre*, by L. Tuetey, 3 vols., Paris, 1912–20. For the modern period there is: *Inventaire des archives conservées au service historique de l'Etat-major de l'armée (Archives modernes)*, by M. Fabre, J.-C. Devos, A. Cambier and L. Garros, 1954.

The records of Overseas Territories (Section *Outre-Mer*) are being reclassified and cannot easily be consulted. In the reading room there is an analytical inventory of the *correspondance générale* running from 1790 to 1835 with a gap from 1805 to 1815.

Mémoires et reconnaissances

1105. Collected memoranda about Africa and America, 1720–85 (e.g., **1209**
report on importance of the fortress of Anamabou, 1780).

1675. Notes on the African coast, n.d.   **1210**

Report on African trade including indigo, gold and slaves, n.d.   **1211**

Notes on the island of Los and the approaches to Sierra Leone, n.d.   **1212**

Description of the English forts and establishments from the R. Gambia **1213**
to the R. Volta, including Fort James, 1784.

Sea routes off the West African coast, including Cape Palmas, Apollonia, **1214** Grand Popo and Whydah, 1784.

1847. Extract from a history of the Spahis of Senegal, which includes some **1215** comments on the native tribes and chiefs in the regions of Futa, etc., 1843–71.

Archives modernes

B 8. West Indies and Africa, 1792–1812

1. Contains *inter alia*, Senegal correspondence, 1801–9.   **1216**

X. Series concerning colonial troops

48. In, *inter alia*, Senegal and Goree, 1815–25.   **1217**

50. Same, 1818.   **1218**

102. Same, 1814–26.   **1219**

Ministry of Foreign Affairs

Ministère des Affaires Etrangères, Quai d'Orsay, Paris VIIe

The reading room is open each afternoon from 2 to 7 p.m. except for the week after Easter and from 14 July to 31 August.

The section of these archives containing European political and commercial documents is open for historical research down to 1914; that containing political correspondence, consular and commercial correspondence and memoranda concerning countries outside Europe down to 1890; that relating to the financial affairs of the Ministry down to 1839; and that consisting of the dossiers of individuals down to 1815. An inventory of the political correspondence can be consulted in the reading room: *Etat numérique des fonds de la correspondance politique de l'origine à 1871*, Paris, 1936. This volume is in three parts: the first relates to documents from the beginning until 1848; a supplement covers the the years 1848 to 1871; and a third section deals with consular political corres- pondence. There is a separate continuation which covers the years 1871 to 1896: *Etat numérique de la correspondance politique 1871–1896*, in two parts: *Correspon- dance politique* and *Correspondance politique des colonies.* This list generally gives only the numbers and dates of the documents and the Minister to whom they were addressed but sometimes includes the names of the correspondents. The *consular* political correspondence is listed according to the countries of origin and subdivided according to place: i.e. *correspondance politique des consuls.* It is difficult to find references to West Africa, and such as have been discovered are concerned with diplomatic negotiations and contain almost no local informa-tion.[1] By far the greatest number of relevant documents are to be found in the series *Mémoires et documents*, of which the inventory is detailed but for the greater part still in manuscript. A more useful series for the history of West Africa is the consular *commercial* correspondence, of which there is a list: *Etat numérique de la correspondance consulaire et commerciale de 1793–1901*,[2] arranged according to the countries in which France maintained consuls and of which the entries under Sierra Leone are the most rewarding.

CONSULAR COMMERCIAL CORRESPONDENCE
Correspondance commerciale

Sierra Leone I: 1848–66

(The French consul in Sierra Leone resided at Ste. Marie-de-Bathurst.)   **1220**

E.g., *011*. Note on the peoples of Malagassea in Sierra Leone.

015. Note on the island of Sherbro, 1855.

126. Description of consul's settlement of quarrel between French captain and native chief of tribe of Mellacouries.

031. Specimens of *ignanes* sent to France to take the place of potatoes.

32. State of navigation in Bathurst.

37 and *39*. Reports on an epidemic of yellow fever, 1859.

The greater part of the documents are concerned with such matters as ship-wrecks, difficulties with cargoes, quarrels about the payment of dues etc.

E.g., *114*. Letter from a chief of Mellacourie, Almami Sanessi, inviting the consult to visit him, 1864.

115. Quarrels between the natives of river Kittam and Gallinas and those of Boom and Bullum, 1863.

125. Letter from Louis H. Tucker, J. Ankafarnar, Bar Peter, chiefs of Seabar in Sherbro asking for French help, 1863.

128. Letter from Morey Saliah, chief of Carsery about deliveries made by him of palm oil etc., 1863.

133. Letter from trader Tallam Tscham protesting about the theft of his goods, 1863.

135. Papers concerning annoyance of traders by natives, 1864.

139. Letter from traders in Rio Pongo, n.d.

170b. Long, and detailed report on the situation on the Gambia and Sierra Leone with comments on the different native peoples, religion, politics, revenue, etc. with maps, 1864.

172. Despatch about trade of English and French in Sierra Leone, 1864.

Sierra Leone 2: 1867–77.   **1221**

Sierra Leone 3: 1881–6.   **1222**

Sierra Leone 4: 1887–1901.   **1223**

[1] For example those which are cited by A. Delcourt: *La France et les Etablissements français au Sénégal entre 1713 et 1763*, Dakar, 1952.

[2] Consular archives from before 1793 are conserved in the Archives Nationales, where they are listed: *Répertoire numérique manuscrit de la sous-série B1 (Affaires étrangères)*, see p. 8 above.

Mémoires et documents

10. *Afrique et colonies françaises I:* 1695–1779   **1224**
   E.g., Historical sketch of West African coast, 1682.
   Memorandum on the trade of Senegal, 1695.
   Regulations of trade with Guinea, some printed, 1716–50.
   Memoranda on the French establishments of Senegal and Guinea, 1750.
   Papers on Goree and the Compagnie des Indes, by M. de Silhouette, 1758.
   Account sheet of the Compagnie royale d'Afrique, 1760–70.
   Extracts from letters by M. Poncet on the situation in Goree, 1764.
   Observations on the trade of the Gambia, 1765.
   Instructions to Ménager about Goree, memoranda on the Compagnie d'Afrique, 1775.
   On Arguin and Portendic; on the gum trade; on Goree, 1778.
   Letter by Christophe de Beaumont, Bishop of Paris, about a missionary from Africa who sought help, 1778.
   State of the garrison of Fort Louis, Senegal; memoranda and correspondence by MM. Paris, Genet, and Lauzun, 1778–9.
   (352 folios, some printed, one map.)

11. *Afrique II:* 1780–1822   **1225**
   E.g., Memoranda on Senegal, 1780–1819.
   Papers on the mines of Bambouk, 1780.
   Papers on the trade of the River Gambia, 1780.
   Documents on the island of Arguin etc. by David, Millet, Gougenot, J.-A. d'Einsiedel, Durand, Mollien, etc., 1780.
   Correspondence of the Count of Repentigny, governor of Senegal, 1784–5.
   Correspondence of Sieur Durand, director of the Compagnie de Sénégal, 1785.
   Treaties between Durand and the marabouts of Armankour, Hamet Moktar, King of the Bracknas, and Ali Koury, King of the Trarzas, 1785.
   Regulations of the Société de l'Afrique intérieure, *An X.*
   Memorandum of the Société coloniale philanthropique of Senegambia, 1817.
   Itinerary from Constantine to Tafilet and Timbuctoo by J.-D. Delaporte, 1822.
   (451 folios, some printed.)

12. *Afrique et colonies françaises III:* 1670–1790   **1226**
   E.g., Reception of the ambassador of the King of Ardres, 1670.
   Description of the capture of Goree from the Dutch by the Comte d'Estrées, 1647.[1]
   Royal confirmation of the privileges of the Compagnie des Indes et Sénégal, 1679.

[1] Several of these documents have been published by M. G. Saint-Yves: 'Les campagnes de Jean d'Estrées dans la mer des Antilles (1676–1678)' in *Bulletin de géographie historique et descriptive*, Paris, 1899.

Memoranda about Dutch pretensions in Cape Verde; description by
Ducasse of events in Goree; confirmation of the privileges of the Com-
pagnie de Sénégal, 1683–5.
Letters patent establishing a new Compagnie de Sénégal, 1698.
Conditions of the slave trade, 1698.
Plan of the factories of the Compagnie de Sénégal in 1701.
Vessels sailing to the concession, 1709–17.
Memoranda on Arguin, 1735.
Plan for regulations about Portendic, 1736.
Memoranda on trade of Senegal by M. de Fulvy, 1736–7.
Condition of the forts of the Compagnie d'Afrique, 1749–51.
Reports on the annoyance of French trade by the English, 1750–1.
Correspondence about Cape Corse, 1715.
Campaign of de Glandeville, n.d.
Memoranda on the trade of the Guinea Coast, by Rouillé, 1751–2.
Report on the islands of Bissao in 1775 and 1790.
(388 folios, some printed.)

E.g., containing memorandum of the tribunal of Goree on the importance of its taking possession of neighbouring territories, 1848. Note on

the trade of Albréda, 1848–51. Demand by English for Bathurst; plan to create a consulate there, 1849, 1850. Rio Nuñez affairs; Belgian plans to establish posts there, 1848, 1850. Affairs concerning Casamance; quarrels with Portuguese there, 1850.

46. Senegal and dependencies, 1852–5.   **1247**

47. Same, 1856–67.   **1248**

48. ,,   1868–75.   **1249**

49. ,,   1876–8.   **1250**

50. ,,   1879–82.   **1251**

51. *French establishments in the Gulf of Guinea*, 1838–62. Various corres- **1252** pondence, etc.

52. Same, 1863.   **1253**

53. ,,   1864–8.   **1254**

54. ,,   1869–76.   **1255**

55. *British possessions on the West African coast*, 1819–65, Lagos, Sierra **1256** Leone, and Boulam.

    E.g., Note on contents of the volume: occupation of islands of Los by English, 1819. Blockade of the port of Gallinas and coast from Camalay to Cape Monte, 1827–8. Trade in guano on coast, 1844. Establishment of English coaling station on Prince's Island, 1844. Human sacrifices in Calabar, 1847 (copy of letter about sacrifices made on death of royal person, printed in English newspaper). Numerous papers about English, French and Portuguese rivalry in Sherbro, etc.

56. British possessions: Sierra Leone and the Gambia, 1866–80.   **1257**

57. Same affair of Mellacourie, Scarcies, and Matacong, conference of **1258** Paris and Anglo-French convention, 28 June 1882.

58. Congo and Gabon, 1839–81. Various.   **1259**

59. Congo, 1882. Mission of Brazza.   **1260**

60. Liberia, 1843–80.   **1261**

74. 1843–55 (e.g., report on French posts which should be established on **1262** the West African coast, 1843; report on French possessions there, 1844. Report on Gulf of Guinea. (n.d.).   **1263**

76. *French establishments in Gulf of Guinea*, 1877–9   **1264**
    E.g., Correspondence with, *inter alia*, French ambassador in London about Dahomey, Kotonou, Assini. Creation of vice-consulate in Whydah and affair concerning protectorate of the King of Porto Novo. Occupation of Kétenon by the English, 1879. Correspondence with the Ministries of Marine and Commerce, the French ambassador in London, Maison Régis, about Dahomey, 1877–9. Blockade of Dahomey by English. Treaty between the English and Dahomeans, 1877. Treaty between the French and the Dahomeans, 1878. Papers about the cession of Kotonou to France. Dutch attempts to recruit workers in Assini, 1878. Delimitation of Assiniean territory, 1877. Plan for a Portuguese blockade of Dahomean coast. Papers about creation of consulate in Whydah, 1878. Letters about troubles with King Tofa, n.d.

77. *French establishments in Gulf of Guinea*, 1880–2   **1265**
    E.g., Correspondence with the Ministry of Marine, and the French
    vice-consul in Whydah etc. about Dahomey, Kotonou, Porto Novo
    and the Popos, 1880–2. Difficulties with England in the Gulf of Guinea.
    Plan for exchanging territories, 1880. Negotiations with England on the
    delimitation of Assini, 1880–2. Re-establishment of French protectorate
    in Porto Novo, 1882. Mission of Captain Mattei to Niger and Benue,
    1882.

78. *French establishments in Gulf of Guinea*, 1883   **1266**
    E.g., Correspondence with the Ministry of Marine, the Resident in
    Porto Novo and in Assini about Grand-Bassam, Assini, Kotonou,
    Porto Novo. Establishment of French protectorate of the Popos, Porto
    Seguro and Agwey. Reorganization of Gold Coast and Gabon.

79. *French establishments in Gulf of Guinea*, 1884   **1267**
    E.g., Mixed commission about the frontiers of Assini. Papers about
    Porto Novo, the Popos and Kotonou. Incident on island of Agnégué.
    Reorganization of French possessions in Guinea.

80. *Gulf of Guinea*, May–December 1884   **1268**
    E.g., Papers concerning Porto Novo, Popos, Kotonou, Agnégué,
    Porto Seguro, Dahomey, Assini, Gridgi. Occupation of Appa by the
    English. Treaties with Noobok, King of Akapless. Treaties with the
    Apoutous. Treaties with Malimba. Report on German ambitions in
    West Africa.

81. *Gulf of Guinea*, January–August 1885   **1269**
    E.g., Papers concerning Dahomey, Porto Novo, Popos, Kotonou,
    Porto Seguro, Agwey. Treaty with the Ouatchis.

82. *Gulf of Guinea*, September–December 1885   **1270**
    E.g., Papers concerning Dahomey, Porto Novo, Popos, Assini,
    Kotonou. Conflict with Portuguese in Dahomey, incident of Gridgi.
    Abandonment of Gridgi and Abanaguem by the Germans.

83. *Gulf of Guinea*, 1886–7   **1271**
    E.g. Papers concerning Dahomey, Porto Novo, Popos, Gridgi,
    Kotonou, Porto Seguro, Assini.
    Declarations by chiefs of Sekko and Djetta, 1886.
    French protectorate of Abanaguem and Agoué, 1886.
    Information about the Ouatchis, 1886.
    Treaties with the Thiakba, l'Indenié, 1887.
    Register containing copies of despatches and telegrams.
    fo. 22. Details about troubles between the Assini, natives of Grand
    Bassam and the Ebrié and with native chief Amangoua in the river
    Akba area; much about diplomatic difficulties with Germans in Porto
    Seguro and Petit Popo; details about French merchants in Porto Seguro
    and German commercial rivalry.
    fo. 51. Copy of declaration by which chiefs of Djetta, depending on
    King of Agoué, recognized French protection and describing the exact
    dimensions of this territory.
    fo. 53. Declaration of the chiefs of Sekko to the same effect and the
    acceptance of France as their protector.

fo. 139. Names given.

fo. 64. Copy of letter sent by King Mensah to the Germans asking for protection, 1886.

fo. 143. Letter in Spanish from King Tofa of Porto Novo, with translation, 1886.

fo. 148. Description of situation in Whydah and Porto Novo, 1886.

fo. 212. Sketch map of Grand Bassam.

fo. 279. Copy of treaty with Ebriés of Grand Bassam. Most of this volume is concerned with the purely diplomatic affairs of Portugal, France, Germany and England. There is hardly any material on the countries themselves.

84. Senegal and dependencies, 15, 1883–4   **1272**

E.g., Information about Mellacourie, Southern rivers, Cape Blanc, Futa-Jalon, Casamance; exchanges in Gambia, 1883. Report on fishing off Cape Blanc, 1883–4. Copy of treaties with Bramaya, Dahedougou. Description of the peoples of Casamance, Lakata, Marcabougon. Report on incident in Casamance. Papers about conflict with Portuguese in Zéguichov, 1884.

85. Senegal and dependencies, 16, 1885–7   **1273**

E.g., Reports on Senegal, southern rivers, Mellacourie, Forrecarea, Futa-Jalon, Arguin, Portendic, Cape Blanc, Timbuctoo. Military operations against Samory by Lt.-Col. Galliéni, 1886–7. Conflict with Portuguese in Casamance, 1886. Question of exchanging Gambia for the southern rivers, 1886. Report on the Trarzas of Rip, Badibou and Salorim, 1886–7. Binger mission to Niger, 1887. Treaties with the Nyamina, Saloum, Rip, Camiah, Sokoto, 1885–7.

86. British possessions in West Africa, 4, 1883–8   **1274**

E.g., English annexations and Anglo-French relations concerning Mellacourie, Lower Niger, Gambia. Report on journey of M. Brun to Ashanti country. English occupation between the R. Gallinas and Mannoh. Mission to King of Segou in Sierra Leone. Letters from Colonna da Secca, consul in Lagos. English protectorate on Niger, 1885–6. Anglo-German agreement about the basin of the river Benue, 1886. Report on affairs in Gambia and Bas-Saloum. English expedition to Toubakouta, 1887.

87–94. Gabon and Congo, 1883–7   **1275**

95. German possessions in West Africa, 1884, 1884–7.   **1276**

E.g., Delimitation of Franco-German boundaries. Report on Nachtigal. Affairs in Dubréka, Popos, Porto Seguro.

96. German possessions in West Africa (2), 1884–7: expedition.   **1277**

E.g., Papers about a German firm, Colin & Co., which suddenly appears in French territory in Dubréka area. *fo. 76.* Treaty between French and chief Balé-Demba. (This volume is otherwise occupied with diplomatic negotiations.)

121. Liberia 2, 1886–92   **1278**

Chiefly concerning the delimitation of Franco-Liberian frontiers.

122. Senegal and dependencies, 1886–9, A   **1279**
    E.g., Papers concerning the French protectorate of Haut-Niger.
Treaties with Samory and chief of Nyamina, 1886. Treaties with
Ahmadou, King of Segou, 1887 etc. Troubles in the Dubréka, campaign
in the Sudan. Recruitment of workers in Senegal for Guyane. Affairs of
Mellacourie and Scarcies. Concessions of Ollivier de Sanderval in the
Upper Niger etc. Treaties with Futa-Jalon. Treaty with Zhieba,
King of Kenedougou, 1888. Report for year 1889.

123. Senegal and dependencies, 1890   **1280**
    E.g., Treaties with Samory. Affair of Senegalese fort at Kaedi. Hostili-
ties in the Sudan. Troubles with Trarzas.

124. Senegal and dependencies, Affairs of the Southern Rivers   **1281**
    E.g., Plan for a railway from Mellacourie to Niger, 1892. Treaties
with the Maures, Trarzas and Braknas. Information about the Sudan,
the circle of Nioro, Casamance, Mellacourie, 1893. Troubles in French
Guinea and with Samory, 1894.

125. French possessions in the Gulf of Guinea, 13, 1888–90   **1282**
    E.g., Affairs of Porto Novo including an agreement with governor of
Lagos. Treaty with Cosroë and chiefs of Grand Bassam, Assini etc., 1888.
Affairs concerning Dahomey, Porto Novo and Popos. Papers concern-
ing Boudoukou; customs system of Gold Coast. Delimitation of Assini,
1889. Two notes on Ivory Coast. Letter from Catholic mission in
Abberkuta, 1890.

126. French possessions in the Gulf of Guinea, 14, Dahomey. Report on Ballot's **1283**
    expedition to Abomey.

127. French possessions in the Gulf of Guinea, 15, 1891–4, Dahomey   **1284**
    E.g., Ballot's expedition to Abomey. Treaty of 3 October, 1890.
Report on the importation of arms. Portuguese fort at Whydah. French
policy in Lower Niger area of Benue. Note about Boudoukou and on
recent treaties in Ivory Coast, 1891. Binger's mission in Boudoukou,
Kong, Diammala. Treaty with the latter, 1892. Establishment of the
French protectorate of Dahomey. Portuguese evacuation of forts of
Ajuda and Whydah, 1893. Treaties with Kings of Abomey, Allada and
the Baribas, 1894.
    87–101. Documents concerning the delimitation of the Hispano-French **1285**
    territories in West Africa.

    114–119. Documents relating to the Anti-Slavery Conference of **1286**
    Brussels, 1889–91.

128. British possessions on the West African coast, 5, 1888–9   **1287**
    E.g., Viard expedition to Abberkuta. Treaty with the Egbas. Charter
of the Royal Africa Company, 1888. Description of the delimitation of
English-French possessions of Porto Novo and Lagos; Assini and Gold
Coast; southern rivers and Sierra Leone, Senegal, Casamance, and
Gambia, 1889.

Archives of Ministry of French Overseas Territories

Archives nationales, Section Outre-Mer, 27 rue Oudinot, Paris VIIe

This archive is open to the public from Monday to Friday from 9.30 a.m. to
midday, and from 2.30 to 5.30 p.m., and on Saturdays from 9.30 a.m. to 12,
on the presentation of such credentials as an ambassadorial letter, or written
permission from the Ministry of Foreign Affairs.

The archives include only the records of the central administration of the
colonies, while those of the various local administrative bodies remain in the
colonies themselves. For a long period all colonial records in France remained
in the Ministry of the Marine as the colonies were administered by it, and it was
only in 1894 that a Ministry was created to deal particularly with the colonies
(an attempt to do this having been made in 1860 but having lasted only two
years). Most of the colonial archives of the period before 1789 were then
transferred to the *Archives Nationales*, where they still remain; for West African
documents the date of division is however 1814. At this point the new classification of the Ministry of Colonies begins, although two series retain the old:
namely the *Série A : Actes du pouvoir souverain* which still continues and *Série B:
Correspondance ministérielle* which includes, in chronological order, copies of all
letters received from the colonial offices, which runs from the beginning (*c.*
1660) to 1860. It must however be noted that for the period before 1858 copies
only of documents of *Série A* were sent to the Ministry of Colonies, while the
originals remained in the archives of the Marine, where they form the *Série
Marine A*. As not all the documents were copied and some copies were lost, the
Série Marine A is more complete than the *Série Colonies A*.

Many of the documents in *Série A*, especially for the period after 1789, have been published in the *Collection des Lois, Décrets, Ordonnances et Règlements* of Duvergier; the *Moniteur*; the *Annales maritimes et coloniales* (from 1809–15 to 1847); the *Bulletin officiel de la Marine* (from 1848 onwards); the *Bulletin officiel de la Marine et des Colonies*, until 1854. All these publications contain tables, and it is easy to find information in them. For the Revolutionary period many relevant texts have been published in the *Recueil des Lois relatives à la Marine et aux colonies*, Paris, 1789/91–1806. The publication of such texts from the period before 1789 is more exceptional, but some may be found in Isambert, Jourdan, and Decrusy *Recueil général des anciennes lois françaises*, 29 vols., Paris, 1822–33. *Série B* contains two or more volumes for each year, one entitled *Colonies* and the other *Autres Lieux*. Two series relating to the period before 1814 only are *Série C: correspondance générale* which includes copies of all correspondence received, including reports and many other documents classified by geographical areas (e.g. *Série C 6* relates to West Africa), and *Série E: personnel ancien* contains the personal dossiers of all non-military and non-marine colonial agents.

The modern series of colonial records (i.e. for West Africa after 1814) which are conserved in the rue Oudinot, are classified according to geographical area, with one common series, for that continent: *Afrique*. Each is subdivided into groups of documents concerning particular subjects, each of which is given a Roman numeral. These series together form the continuation of the old *Série C*, which had become much too bulky. The modern series is completed by the continuation of the old *Série E: personnel ancien*, by *Série E: personnel moderne*. Access to these series is seldom granted.

A separate Series, *Fortifications*, which includes not only documents concerning buildings, but many other memoranda and reports on a great variety of subjects, may also be consulted in the reading room in the rue Oudinot. The records are open there for the period 1815 to 1914. For the period 1910 to 1914 they have not yet been catalogued. There is a very detailed card index: *Afrique—Ancienne série C*.[1]

The index is divided into the following sections for each area:
    I. General correspondence—'in' and 'out' letters
    II. General reports, publications, and exhibitions
    III. Exploration, missions, and travels
    IV. Territorial expansion and native politics
    V. Military expeditions
    VI. Relations with foreign powers
    VII. General and municipal administration
    VIII. Justice
    IX. Finance
    X. Cults
    XI. Police, hygiene, and public assistance
    XII. Works and communications

[1] These documents have been extensively used by C. Schefer: *La France moderne et le problème colonial*, Paris, 1907.

Série C

[1] The series Afrique I–III, and Sénégal I–XX, have been extensively used by G. Hardy in *La mise en valeur du Sénégal de 1817 à 1854*, Paris, 1921.

15. Gabon, 1839–81.   1319
16. Gabon, 1882–6.   1320

Afrique II. General reports
1. Plans for establishments, 1830.   1321
2. Plans for establishments, 1831–60.   1322
3. Plans for establishments, 1861–19—.   1323
4. General reports, 17th–20th century.   1324
5. General reports, 1886–19—.   1325
5bis. Scheme for an international conference to improve the lot of native   1326
Africans, 1897.
6. Meteorological documents, 1901.   1327

Afrique III. Exploration and missions
1. Papers about, *inter alia*, Boditch, leader of the English mission to the   1328
Ashanti, 1830.
3. Badia. Journey in Africa, political report, 1801–7.   1329
4. Badia. Journey in Africa, political report, 1805–7.   1330
5. Badia. Original notes about his travels in Africa and Asia, 1803–8. 1331
8. Badia, 1817–21.   1332
9. Magnan. Plan for exploring the Niger, 1864.   1333
14. Mizon mission, 1893.   1334
15. Mizon mission, 1890–2.   1335
16. Mizon mission, 1892–3, including report on events in Upper Benue,   1336
1894.
17. Mizon mission, 1892–9.   1337
18. Further French missions, 1892–5.   1338
19. Monteil mission, 1893–6.   1339
20. Monteil mission, 1893–6.   1340
21. Monteil mission, 1893–6.   1341
22. Monteil mission, including register of correspondence and diary of   1342
travels, 1894–5.
23. Monteil mission, 1894–5.   1343
24. Foreign exploration, 1890–5.   1344
25.   ,,   ,,   1895–7.   1345
26.   ,,   ,,   1895–7.   1346
27.   ,,   ,,   1895–8.   1347
28.   ,,   ,,   1896–1905.   1348
29.   ,,   ,,   1897–1902.   1349
30.   ,,   ,,   1898–1902.   1350

Afrique VI

This is occupied by diplomatic affairs and particularly with the delimitation of
territories belonging to the European powers, and details from it have therefore
been omitted. Sections VII–XI do not appear in *Afrique*.

Afrique XII. Public works and communications

A O F (*Afrique occidentale française*)

Dahomey I. 1–19. General correspondence, from 1889

Dahomey II. 1–4. Memoranda, from 1890

Dahomey III. 1–9. Exploration

Dahomey IV. 1–5. Territorial expansion and native politics, from 1889

Dahomey V. 1–12. Military expeditions, 1889–95

Dahomey VI. 1–5. Diplomatic affairs, from 1889

---

[1] Although the latest date for which documents can be seen is officially 1907, more have quite frequently been added and are open to 1914.
[2] This includes instructions to colonial governors, despatches etc.

3. Papers about the arts, including some on meteorology. **1549**

4. Catholic and Presbyterian missions. **1550**

5. Papers about Arab schools. **1551**

6. Papers about the arts. **1552**

7. Papers about monuments, to be erected. **1553**

8. Papers about, *inter alia*, the apostolic-vicariate of Tchad. **1554**

Gabon XI. 1–22. Police and hygiene, 1859–1919

1. Papers about the organization of the police. **1555**
E.g., XI, 1: (1) Request by the Portuguese of St. Thomas for the extradition of eight natives, wanted for murder, who had fled to Gabon. (2) Papers about the expulsion of two English merchants, Robert and William Walker, from the village of Glass, for attacking the son of the chief of a village between Glass and Libreville. (3) Complaints by natives against various whites for violence. (4) Papers about the murder of a child. (5) Troubles in Mingué-Mingué. (6) Papers about the execution of a native bandit at Grand Bassam.

2. Papers about cabarets etc. **1556**

3. Papers about foreigners. **1557**

4. Papers about fires. **1558**

5. Papers about fines. **1559**

6–9. Papers about hygiene. **1560**

10–15. Papers about foreigners, deportations, personal dossiers, penal **1561**
regulations, etc.

16–17. Hygiene. **1562**

18. Public assistance. **1563**

19–22. Papers about the Gabon–Congo. **1564**

Gabon XII. 1–29. Public works and communications, 1859–1907

1–5. Public works. **1565**

6. Water. **1566**

7. Navigation and ports, lighthouse of Libreville. **1567**

8. Roads and railways. **1568**

9–11. Posts and telegraphs. **1569**

12–26. Gabon–Congo. **1570**

27. Navigation. **1571**

28. Navigation on the Upper Ubangi. **1572**

29. Navigation of the Kanem-Chad. **1573**

Gabon XIII. 1–24. Agriculture, commerce and industry, 1859–1912

1. Commerce. **1574**

2bis. Agriculture, including medicinal plants. **1575**

Gabon XIV. 1–3. Labour, 1860–1910

Gabon XV. 1–91. Dossiers of individual firms, indicating each name dates, 1859–1912

Gabon XVI 1–16. Troops and marine, 1859–1910

Includes general papers: information about the recruitment of native soldiers; personnel, etc.

Includes reports of ordinary general inspections and some special missions, as Verrier, Blanchard, Bouchaut: commission to investigate the Congo.

Includes correspondence, statistical reports on trade, industry and agriculture, 1869–70.

Goree IV. 1–3. Territorial expansion and native politics

Goree XI. Police etc., 1855–9.

Goree XIII. Trade, 1845–58.

Goree XV. Private firms, 1852–8   1601
These entries contain only one or two reports each.

Guinea I. 1–9. General correspondence, 1889–1902   1602
These papers consist of correspondence, despatches and instructions from
the Lieutenant-Governor of the Southern Rivers.

Guinea II. 1–3. Memoranda, publications etc., 1889–95   1603
Guinea III. 1–5. Exploration and missions, 1889–92
1. Papers about exploration in the Futa-Jalon, 1900.   1604
2, 3. Same for Le Barigui and Futa-Jalon, 1900.   1605
3bis. Same for Lamadou, 1892.   1606
5. Papers about communications between Konakry and the river Niger, 1607
1897–8.

Guinea IV. 1–7. Territorial expansion and native politics, 1889–95
1. Papers about the Rio Nuñez region and relations with the king, Dinah- 1608
Salifou, 1889–95.
2. Information concerning Pongo, 1889–95.   1609
3. Same for Dubréka, 1889–95; relations with King Balé-Siaka, 1889–95. 1610
4. Same for Mellacourie, 1889–95.   1611
5. Same for Futa-Jalon, 1889–95.   1612
6. Papers concerning treaties.   1613

Guinea V. Military expeditions, 1889–95   1614
Guinea VI. Diplomatic affairs, 1889–95   1615
Guinea VII. General administration, 1889–95   1616
Guinea VIII. Justice, 1889–93   1617
Guinea IX. Finance, 1889–95   1618
Guinea X. Cults, 1889–95   1619
Guinea XI. Police, 1889–95   1620
Guinea XII. 1–8. Public works, 1889–95   1621
E.g., *3.* Plan of Konakri, n.d. *6.* Reports on the railway project
between Konakri and the Niger.

Guinea XIII. 1–8. Agriculture, trade, and industry, 1889–95
1, 2. General.   1622
3. Reports on palm oil etc.   1623
4. Reports on coffee, beef and guano.   1624
5, 6. Reports on wood and arms.   1625
7. Reports on rubber, 1902–3.   1626
8. Statistics, 1885–1900.   1627

12. Staple, 1895–   **1659**
16. Treasury, 1895–   **1660**
17. Currency, 1895–   **1661**
18. Annual budgets, 1895–   **1662**
19. Papers about Rénard.   **1663**

Ivory Coast X. 1–2. Cults and education, 1889–95
1. General papers.   **1664**
2. Local education and education in the capital.   **1665**

Ivory Coast XI. 1–10. Police, hygiene, 1889–1904   **1666**

Ivory Coast XII. 1–11. Works and communications, 1889–95
1. General.   **1667**
2. Public buildings.   **1668**
3. Ports.   **1669**
4. Posts.   **1670**
5. General, 1895–   **1671**
6. Administrative buildings, 1895–   **1672**
7. Railways, 1895–   **1673**
8. Coastal navigation, 1895–   **1674**
9. Ports and quays, 1895–   **1675**
10. Wharf of Grand Bassam, 1895–   **1676**
11. Steamers, posts, 1895–   **1677**
12. Telegraphs, 1895–   **1678**

Ivory Coast XIII. 1–5. Agriculture, commerce and industry, from 1889
1. General.   **1679**
2. Forests, palm oil, coffee.   **1680**
3. Arms, gold dust.   **1681**
4. Ship-wrecks.   **1682**
5. Agriculture, commerce and industry various, from 1895. **1683**

Ivory Coast XIV.1–3. Labour recruitment and slavery, 1890–7 **1684**
Ivory Coast XV. 1–8. Papers about private firms
1. General.   **1685**
2–8. Papers about private firms.   **1686**

Ivory Coast XVI. 1–9. Troops and naval forces
1. General.   **1687**
1bis. Health.   **1688**
2. Senegalese riflemen.   **1689**

[1] The series Senegal I, II, III, IV, XIII, XV have been used extensively by E. Saulnier: *La Compagnie de Galam au Sénégal*, Paris, 1921. The archives of the company, which should have been put into the government archives in Dakar, cannot be traced.

[2] Senegal was cut off from France during the Napoleonic wars and only reoccupied from 1815 onwards.

[3] Instructions printed by C. Schefer: *Instructions générales données de 1763 à 1870 aux gouverneurs et ordonnateurs des établissements français en Afrique occidentale*, vol. I, 1763–1831, vol. II, 1831–70, Paris, 1921.

[4] These instructions, which often describe the colony and its dependencies in some detail, continue down to 1895. There are 98 numbers in all.

Map of the St. Louis region, 1858.   **1711**

Map of the area between the Senegal and Saloum rivers, 1862.   **1712**

Senegal III. Exploration

1. Expeditions by Orogery-Estray, de Chastelus, Gray, Mollien, 1815–19.   **1713**

2. Same, Grandiu, 1819–20; Bodin, 1821–2; Sauvigny, 1822.   **1714**

3. Same, De Beaufort, 1823–8;[1] Perrollet, 1825; Plagne, 1825; Blanc, 1827;   **1715**
Danglès, 1828.[2]

4. Same, Mouttet, 1828–9; Duranton, 1828–30.   **1716**

5. Caillié etc., 1838; Bouët, 1839; Fleuriot de Langle, 1841.   **1717**

6. De Langle, 1842; Lahalle, 1842; Kerhallet, 1842; Huart etc., 1843.   **1718**

7. Pigeard, 1846; Méguet, 1846; Raffenel, 1845–7; Rousseau, 1849.   **1719**

8. Lagorgne, 1850; Rey, 1851; Hecquart, 1849–51; Brossard de Coligny,   **1720**
1857; Gaude, 1859.

9. Braouezec, 1862; Poisson, 1863; Mage-Quintin, 1863–6.   **1721**

10. Besnard, 1872; Canard, 1876; Soller, n.d.   **1722**

10bis. Galliéni, including relations with Ahmadou, 1879–81.   **1723**

11. Labrouche, Lecard, Bayol, Colin, Brosselard, Peroz, Olivier, 1880–7.   **1724**

12. Le Gabès, Raffenel, Arnoux, Jacomy, Muller, Audéoud, Dr. Colin,   **1725**
1886–8.

13. Brosselard-Faidherbe, Binger, Colin, astronomical mission, 1889–95.   **1726**
E.g., 1890. (a) Papers about Emile Serraut's trip to the Upper Senegal
and Western Sudan, 1888. Letter from Faidherbe to the minister who
accompanied him on one of his explorations and took photographs.
Letter from the administrator of Casamance to the governor of Senegal.
Papers about the attempts of the native chiefs round Madina against
Faidherbe. Papers on the expenses of the Binger expedition. Extracts
from an account of a trip to Benin and Grand Bassam. Papers about an
astronomical expedition and an eclipse of the sun 1893. Dr. Colin's
mission in 1895.

14. Moreau, Gerardin, Mindray de Roumilly, Ardin d'Elteil, Laplène,
1818–89.   **1727**

17. (b). Viard mission from Dahomey to the middle Niger, 1888.   **1728**

45bis. Military situation in Senegal, 1859–90.   **1729**

Senegal IV.

1. Reoccupation, 1783–1818, Albréda.   **1730**

2. Albréda: general correspondence, 1817–55.   **1731**

---

[1] See C. Faure, 'Le voyage d'exploration de Grant de Beaufort au Sénégal en 1824 et
1825', in *Bulletin de la Section de Géographie*, vol. XXXIV, Paris, 1919.

[2] Some details about Danglès expedition in Casamance and the texts of some treaties
with native chiefs are printed in E. Saulnier, 'Les français en Casamance', in *Revue de
l'histoire des colonies françaises*, Paris, 1914.

E.g., Papers about an expedition to burn villages supporting Trarzas,
1835. Attempts to stop Princess Gimballe in Cayor from obtaining
arms etc. to allow her to prolong her war against the Walo. Raiders
against the merchants of St. Louis, 1834. Papers in Arabic and French
about treaties with the Walo and Bracknas. Extracts from newspapers
about the Walo affair. Documents about prisoners of war, 1835. Descriptions of peace palavers with the Trarzas, 1829.

[1] One letter from the commander of Goree, Hesse, is printed by E. Saulnier, 'Une
réception royale à l'île de Gorée en 1831', in the *Revue d'histoire des colonies françaises*,
Paris, 1918.

68. Senegalese Futa, relations with Abdoul-Boubakar, 1884–90.   **1795**

69. Senegalese Futa, relations with Abdoul-Boubakar, 1890–95.   **1796**

70. Boudou, relations with Ousman-Gassé, 1888–9, and Malick Fouré,   **1797**
1891–5.

71. Futa-Jalon, 1879–95.   **1798**

72. Futa-Jalon, 1894–5.   **1799**

73–96. Soudan, n.d.   **1800**

97. N'Diambour, 1879–95.   **1801**

98. Cayor, 1879–84.   **1802**

99. Cayor, 1885–8.   **1803**

100. Cayor, 1889–95.   **1804**

101. Djoloff: treaties, 1879–95.   **1805**

102. Baol, 1889–95.   **1806**

103. Joal and Portudal, 1879–95.   **1807**

104. Sine and Saloum, 1879–95.   **1808**

105. Rip, 1887–95.   **1809**

106. Casamance; *inter alia*, treaty with King Firdon, 1879–85.   **1810**

107. Casamance; *inter alia*, 1886–91.   **1811**

108. Casamance: relations with Fodé-Kaba, Fodé-Silla, Moussa-Molo,   **1812**
Maugone Leye, 1890–5.

109. Rio Cassini: *inter alia*, occupation by France, 1879–89.   **1813**

110. Rio Nuñez, 1879–90.   **1814**

111. Islands of Alcatraz, 1879–89.   **1815**

112. Rio Pongo, 1879–90.   **1816**

113. Rio Dubréka, from 1880; treaty with Balé-Siaka, 1889.   **1817**

114. Island of Matacong, 1880–9.   **1818**

115. Rio Mellacourie: correspondence about the political situation on the   **1819**
Guinea Coast, 1879–83.

116. Same, 1884–9.   **1820**

117. Scarcies, 1879–87.   **1821**

118. Ivory Coast: *inter alia*, treaties, 1885–9.   **1822**

119. Ivory Coast, 1885–9.   **1823**

120. Benin: treaty with king Amadou de Loko, 1883, 1886–9.   **1824**

121. Porto Novo: relations with King Joffa, 1887.   **1825**

122. Porto Novo: treaty with the chiefs of Ouémé and Joffa, 1887.   **1826**

123. Porto Novo: treaty with the chiefs of Ouémé and Joffa, 1888.   **1827**

124. Porto Novo, correspondence.   **1828**

125. Porto Novo, Popos, 1886–9.   **1829**

126. Cape Blanc and the Bay of Arguin, 1880–95. **1830**

127. Moslem affairs, 1880–95. **1831**

128. Various, 1895–7. **1832**

Senegal VI. Diplomatic affairs (some purely diplomatic files have been omitted)

1e. Commercial relations between the English fort in the Gambia and Senegal, 1838–40. **1833**

2. Portugal, conflicts in Casamance. **1834**

4. England: affairs concerning Portendic, Gambia, Casamance, etc., 1840–60. **1835**

7. England: affairs concerning the rivers Grand and Bolole, commercial relations, 1861–70. **1836**

11. Portugal, commercial relations, 1871–80. **1837**

13. Difficulties of Mellacourie spreading to Sierra Leone, 1881–5. **1838**

16. Includes explorations of Dr. Nachtigal, 1881–5. **1839**

20. Portugal: *inter alia*, conflict at Whydah, 1886–90. **1840**

22. Germany: *inter alia*, delimitation of Togo and Benin, 1886–90. **1841**

23. Expedition to Grand Bassam, 1889; Liberia, 1886–90. **1842**

24. Travels on the coast of Gambia, 1888. **1843**

25. England: *inter alia*, documents about Fodé-Kaba and Fodé-Silla, 1890–5. **1844**

29. Germany: trade in arms, 1890–5. **1845**

Senegal VII. 16. General and municipal administration

1. Administrative organization, 1822–40. **1846**

2. Plans for administrative organization, 1816–40. **1847**

3, 5, 9, 10, 11–20. Same, 1822–40. **1848**

6. Administrative council of Goree, correspondence etc., 1822–7. **1849**

7. Representation in France, 1816–48. **1850**

8. Municipal organization, 1816–40. **1851**

21. Functioning of the services, including register of correspondence with the native chiefs, 1888, 1840–95. **1852**

22–69. General administration, including documents about elections, election lists, general correspondence, municipal elections and administration, budget proposals. **1853**

Senegal VIII. Justice

1, 4, 7, 11, 14, 18, 23, 27. Judicial organization. **1854**

2. Commercial code, 1819. **1855**

3, 6, 9, 10, 13, 16, 17, 20–22, 25, 26, 29. Administration of justice, 1816–95. **1856**

5, 8, 12, 15, 19, 24, 28. Judicial legislation, 1822–95. **1857**

18–24. Papers about the water supply.   **1889**

25–35. Papers about navigation and ports: *inter alia*, Dakar and Rufisque. **1890**

36–38. Roads and bridges.   **1891**

39–75. Papers about, *inter alia*, the Dakar–St. Louis railway.   **1892**

76–80. Papers about, *inter alia*, Ikayes–Niger railway.   **1893**

81–82. Papers about, *inter alia*, Thies–Ikayes railway.   **1894**

83. Papers about various projects.   **1895**

84–90. Papers about posts and telegraphs, steamers.   **1896**

94–109. Papers about navigation and ports, 1815–95.   **1897**

Senegal XIII. Agriculture, trade and industry, 1815–95
  Commerce
1. General memoranda, 1895.   **1898**

2. Papers about the organization of trade, 1851.   **1899**

3. Various reports.   **1900**

4, 5. Papers concerning the Chambers of Commerce.   **1901**

6. Papers about money changers and insurances, and Casamance.   **1902**

7–9. Papers concerning the Compagnie de Galam et Dualo. 1830–5.   **1903**

10. Papers about the trade of Galam, 1849–51.   **1904**

11. Papers about the trade of St. Louis, Goree, Dakar, Rufisque, Casa-   **1905**
mance etc.

12. Reports on Guinea's trade with Sierra Leone, the Ivory Coast and   **1906**
Benin, 1886–9.

13–16. Reports on regional trade and fortified posts, 1841–54.   **1907**

17. Agriculture.   **1908**

18–20. Papers about attempts at colonization, 1818–45.   **1909**

22–23. Experimental plantations, 1854.   **1910**

24–33. Reports about the production of gum, 1815–39.   **1911**

34–38. Reports about the production of cotton, 1816–95.   **1912**

39. Reports about the production of indigo, 1816–95.   **1913**

40–50. Reports about other products, e.g., rice, cereals, rubber, 1815–95.   **1914**

50–53. Reports about fishing, 1825–   **1915**

54–56. Report on the mines of Bambouk, 1815–56.   **1916**

57. Papers about guano production, 1815–95.   **1917**

58–60. Papers about other produce, 1815–95.   **1918**

61–68. Papers about navigation, 1815–95.   **1919**

69. Memoranda about exports to foreign countries, 1839–95.   **1920**

70. Papers concerning foreigners, 1816–95.   **1921**

71. Papers about weights and measures, 1820–95.   **1922**

Senegal XIV. Work and employers, 1818–23

1b, 10. Papers about ships which had been seized for taking part in the slave trade, 1818–32.   **1923**

2–4, 7, 13, 14, 15a–c, 28. Information about the repression of the slave trade, 1818–87.   **1924**

8. Papers about the expedition of Bauden to conclude treaties with West African chiefs, and correspondence on this subject, 1845–8.   **1925**

9. Correspondence about such treaties concluded by the English, 1845–57.   **1926**

12. Papers about the police and the *état civil* of the natives, 1824–51.   **1927**

16, 17. Judicial papers about slavery, 1828–82.   **1928**

18. General questions about the enrolment of African labour for the colonies, 1821–47.   **1929**

19–21. Information about the numbers of slaves, 1823–44.   **1930**

23a–c, 25. Correspondence with the governor of Senegal about African immigration, 1852–62.   **1931**

26–28. Papers about the recruitment of native workers, 1891–5.   **1932**

Senegal XV. Private companies, 1816–95

1, a. Correspondence, b. papers, about the land along the Dakar–St. Louis railway.   **1933**

2–4. Papers about the Société coloniale philanthropique du Cap Vert, 1814–24.   **1934**

5–28. Requests for and concessions of land for setting up various industries.   **1935**

28–34. Papers about the concession and sale of land, 1816–95.   **1936**

Senegal XVI. Troops and naval forces

3–4. General correspondence about native troops, 1819–95.   **1937**

5–18. Further details about personnel etc., 1819–60.   **1938**

19–20. Papers about the artillery, 1825–95.   **1939**

20–27. Papers about the Senegalese riflemen, 1857–95.   **1940**

28–29. Papers about the Spahis.   **1941**

30–42. Papers concerning the maintenance of order, and the supply of the troops, *c.* 1820–90.   **1942**

43–54. Local military posts, 1850–95.   **1943**

55–57bis. Information about military personnel, *c.* 1846–90.   **1944**

58. Troops and naval forces on the Upper River, 1882–90.   **1945**

62–70. Same, 1890–1902.   **1946**

Senegal XVII. 1–32. Provisioning, 1814–1903. These papers consist of lists of food supplies and materials.   **1947**

Senegal XVIII. 1–30. Personnel, 1816–95. These papers consist of annual reports on staff and their salaries.   **1948**

Senegal XIX. 1–14. Control and inspections, 1817–99   **1949**

Senegal XX. 1–8. Statistics, 1821–95. These papers contain reports about   **1950**
agriculture, trade, and industry and some information about the movement of the population.

PLANS AND FORTIFICATIONS[1]

There are three manuscript inventories of this series: numbers 4, 5, 25. All give
details about the author and date of the documents noted, as well as an analysis
of the items, in chronological order, between 1670 and 1880. The documents
include letters, reports, budgets, plans, maps concerning various industrial
matters such as the mining of gold, the local production of various goods, such
as gum, details about the slave trade, treaties with natives, etc. The material is
divided into cartons to which the numbers given here refer.

Inventory no. 4 chiefly concerns Senegal.

Carton 1 no. 4. Memorandum by du Casse about his travels in Guinea, with   **1951**
remarks about trade etc., kingdom by kingdom, 1687–8.

Carton 1 no. 12. Description of a voyage to Guinea made by M. Le Chr.   **1952**
Damon, 1698.

Carton 1 no. 21. Amounts of gum sold by the Compagnie des Indes, giving   **1953**
dates and amounts sold, 1719–21.

Carton 2 nos. 112, 113. Map of part of the west coast of Africa by Givry,   **1954**
1817.

no. 123. Memorandum about the colonization of Senegal by Schmaltz,   **1955**
1818.

Inventory no. 5. Goree, Gold Coast, and Gabon, 1677–1873.

Carton 1 no. 23. Treaties with native chiefs, 1728.   **1956**

Inventory no. 25. Drawings and memoranda about the African coast, con-   **1957**
taining plans and notes about Arguin, Portendic, the Gambia, Sierra
Leone, Elmina, Whydah, Accra etc., 1644–1815.

---

[1] This is a separate series which contains plans and memoranda from the geographical
and commercial point of view: Inventory no. 4, 97 pp.; no. 5, 89 pp.; no. 25, 189 numbers.

Ministry of Marine

Service historique de la Marine, 3 avenue Octave Gréard, Paris VIIe

These archives are open to the public from 9 to 11.30 a.m. and from 2 to 5 p.m. on presentation of a letter from the appropriate ambassador or from the French Ministry of Foreign Affairs.

The centralized archives of the Marine exist only from the time of Colbert. Until then the head of the French navy was the Admiral of France, who was responsible not only for the navy but for the merchant marine, and who was represented by local Admiralty offices.[1] His power was in fact very limited in time and in extent because it applied only to the royal domain: Brittany and Guyenne for example retaining independent jurisdiction in this sphere for a century and a half after their union with the Crown. Material for the history of the colonies therefore may be found not only in the central archives of the Marine but also where the Admiral operated: *les sièges d'Amirauté*. Each area had its own court to decide all matters concerning shipping in that region, and issued passports, received reports on voyages, and so forth.

Before 1669 the affairs of the Marine were administered by two under-secretaries, one for the Levant region and another for the Ponant. Documents continued to be classified according to these two areas even after their adminis-tration had been united. Records concerning West Africa must be sought among those of the Ponant region. Colbert created a separate Marine archive depot in 1699, and its records from before 1870 will be found in the *Archives Nationales*. With a few rare exceptions documents for the period after 1870 are conserved by the *Service historique de la Marine*. These can be supplemented by records from the local depots of the Marine in Brest, Cherbourg, Lorient, Rochefort, and Toulon. The archives are classified in series distinguished by letters of the alphabet, single for the period before 1789 (A to G) and thereafter double (AA-GG). The series in which most information about West Africa may be found are B4 or BB4: *campagnes*, which contain *inter alia* numerous reports from naval personnel on duty off the African coast.[2]

Marine BB4. Campagnes

889. Reports from the naval division on the West African coast, 1868–71.[3] **1958**

902. Minutes of the naval stations in, *inter alia*, West Africa, 1870. **1959**

916. Letters received from, *inter alia*, the Gulf of Guinea, 1870–1. **1960**

949. Letters received from, *inter alia*, the West African coast, 1871–2. **1961**

[1] See, e.g., the records of the Admiralty of La Rochelle.
[2] The typed inventory of these papers may be consulted in the reading room. It contains a few documents which have been omitted from the manuscript inventory by Bourgin (see Marine section in List of the *Archives Nationales*) because they are of the period after 1870.
[3] See also the note to the Marine Section of the National Archives, p. 32.

974. Letters received from, *inter alia,* the West African coast, 1874. This **1962**
volume contains letters from Gabon, Dakar, with details about winds
and so on; reports about the kidnapping of a hostage from Gabon;
reports about a punitive expedition up the River Mondah against Chief
Mackinde; papers about forced labour.

985. Letters received from, *inter alia,* the West African coast, 1875. **1963**

1180. Minutes of the administration of the Gulf of Guinea, 1885. **1964**

1190. Same, 1886. **1965**

1344. Papers about an expedition to the Congo, 1884. **1966**
1364–6: Colonies. These documents consist of methodical collections of
miscellaneous information about the colonies, including newspaper
reports.

1364. Senegal, 1888–94. **1967**
   E.g., contains a report on the military and political situation on the
Anglo-French frontier at Assini. Papers about the French influence in
West Africa. Reports on various missions to French Sudan (by Festing,
Thieba). Papers about the treaty of protection with the Zahayah
country. Reports on the Binger mission. Information about the area
between Porto Novo and the middle Niger. Papers about incidents
in Baol, and the capture of Koudian. Note on English activities in
Porto Novo. Treaty with the chiefs of Cosroë (Grand Bassam), and the
concession of a region to the West of the Upper Niger. Reports about
the Anglo-French frontier in West Africa and incidents at Whydah.
Regulations about the organization of French possessions on the coast.
Reports on Bayol's expedition to Dahomey, and the war against the
latter. Reports on an expedition to the Ivory Coast and the embarkation
of slaves at Whydah. Information about Timbuctoo and Cape Blanc.

1368. Report on Spanish possessions in West Africa. E.g., Note on the **1968**
numbers of troops in the area, 1891. Project for ceding Portuguese
Guinea to France, 1889–90. Report on the English establishment at Cape
Juby. Reports on the English violation of the French protectorate of
Gambia and the delimitation of Gambia, Sierra Leone, Assini, Grand
Bassam and Porto Novo, 1889–94. Report on troubles in Grand Bassam,
and military information about Monrovia's delimitation, 1889–94.
Report on the struggle of Dahomey against Porto Novo, and Portugal's
evacuation of Dahomey, 1890. German treaties with natives in their
possessions declared void. Reports on the slave trade in Togo and the
bombardment of Bitundi by the Germans. Reports on the German
exploration of the Benue and troubles in the Cameroons. Note on the
embarkation of slaves at Whydah, 1889–4. Report on the actions of the
British Niger Company.

1376. Papers about the defence of Senegal, and the defence of Dakar and **1969**
St. Louis, 1885.

1377. Plan for the organization of a postal service between France and the **1970**
West African coast, 1887.

1378. Includes report on the garrison in Senegal, 1887; map of Porto Novo, **1971**
1886; and report on the defences of the harbour of Dakar, 1887.

1386. Report on mistakes in the administration of the Gold Coast and the **1972** stagnation of trade, 1887.

1388. Includes letters from the French Minister of Foreign Affairs about the **1973** delimitation of French, English, and Portuguese possessions in West Africa, 1885; papers about difficulties concerning the treaty made with the King of Dahomey, 1885.

1389. Includes letters of the French Minister of Foreign Affairs concerning **1974** Spanish rights in territory on the Gulf of Guinea, and in the Grand Popo area; papers about Dakar harbour, 1885; report in German about Portuguese explorations in West Africa, 1885.

1390. Includes reports on the possibilities of a treaty with Samory, 1886; **1975** papers about a treaty with the Ouatchis, and on rivalry between the English and Germans on the lower Niger and at Benue, 1886.

1391. Reports on diplomatic negotiations concerning West Africa, 1886. **1976**

1395. Letters of commanders at sea. **1977**
    E.g., p. 5. Reports on Whydah, Lagos, Accra, 1852.
    pp. 417–21. Information about Cape Coast.
    pp. 431–3.   ,,   ,,   St. George Delmina.
    pp. 441–6.   ,,   ,,   Jellah Coffee.
    pp. 467–72.   ,,   ,,   Whydah.
    pp. 473–84.   ,,   ,,   Petit Popo and Grand Popo.
1398.

    p. 574. Notes on the frontiers of Assini, 1884. **1978**
    p. 1121. Report on events in Umculla (Gulf of Guinea).
1399.

    pp. 91, 269. Report on the defence of the coast of Senegal, 1886. **1979**
    pp. 1007, 1027. Reports on Freetown and Elmina, n.d.

1400. Letters from colonial governors in Senegal and French West Africa. **1980**
    E.g., p. 183. Report by the commission set up to study navigation on the upper reaches of the river Niger, 1879.
    p. 253. Project for a fort at Kadei, 1883.
    p. 261. Report on the colony of the Niger, 1884.
    p. 271. Report on an incident between French and Portuguese at Sindoni (Casamance), 1884.
    pp. 273, 343, 357, 367, 391, 413, 427, 437, 445, 449. Papers about the political situation in Senegal and the hostility of the native peoples of the Niger region, 1884.
    p. 375. Difficulties in Futa, 1884.
    p. 399. German activities reported, 1885.
    p. 425. Treaty between Germans and King Prassal about the Cameroons, 1885.
    p. 441. Anglo-French incidents in Apollonia, 1885.
    p. 445. Report on Lagos and Porto Novo, 1885.
    p. 491. Report on difficulties with Ahmadou in Senegal, 1886.
    p. 503. Report on Sierra Leone:
On the establishment in the Gulf of Guinea.
The political situation in Gabon, 1883–4.

1402. Consular correspondence. Includes I/43a. p. 411. Report on the **1981**
support which France should give to Liberia, 1879.

1403. p. 405. Includes report from the French consul in Lagos on the with- **1982**
drawal of English troops, and the French garrison at Porto Novo, 1884.

1405. Includes report by the French Vice-Consul in Sierra Leone. I/43b. **1983**
Report on the movements of war ships, 1885–6.

1409. Includes pp. 491–505, letters from the naval attaché in London. **1984**
Report on the Ashanti, 1883.

1410. Includes pp. 9, 14, letters from the naval attaché in London on the **1985**
Ashanti war, 1884; pp. 61, 77–91, plans and maps of Lagos and Porto
Novo, 1884.

1416. Miscellaneous correspondence (including, p. 136, list of the estab- **1986**
lishments of the house of Manuel frères of Bordeaux, in West Africa,
1885; pp. 137–8, report on the slave trade of Portugal in Dahomey, 1885.

1422. pp. 107–12. Report on atrocities and thieving in the native state of
Samory, 1888.

Typed inventory no. 6

1435. p. 879. Note on the German and Italian workers in Senegal, 1884. **1987**
Inventory no. 7

1619 (152). Letters received from Senegal, 1889–92; Dahomey, 1884–93; **1988**
Haut-Oubanghi and Chari, 1897–1904.

1621 (154). Dossier of various documents concerning Assini and Grand **1989**
Bassam, 1786–1885.

1660, 1663, 1671. Letters received from Senegal etc., 1902. **1990**

1674, 1682. Minutes from Gabon, Senegal, 1904. **1991**

1685, 1692. , ,, ,, ,, 1905. **1992**

1696. ,, ,, ,, ,, 1906. **1993**

1706. ,, ,, ,, ,, 1907. **1994**

1716. ,, ,, ,, ,, 1908. **1995**

1726. ,, ,, ,, ,, 1909. **1996**

1703. Letters received from Gabon and Senegal, 1906. **1997**

1713. ,, ,, ,, ,, ,, ,, 1907. **1998**

1721. ,, ,, ,, ,, ,, ,, 1908. **1999**

1731. ,, ,, ,, ,, ,, ,, 1891–8. **2000**

1820. Includes plan of the Bay of Levrier from the *Recueil des dossiers du* **2001**
Bureau des Mouvements.

1940–5. Reports on the Congo expedition, 1883. Includes letters from the **2002**
governors of Gabon and Senegal; Minutes of despatches to, *inter alia*, the
commander of the Gulf of Guinea, the governor of Senegal, etc.

1942. Inter alia, notes from the commander of the West African squadron, **2003**
1876–83.

1945. Reports from the explorers, La Porte, Le Duc, and Mizon in Gabon   **2004**
and Ogudué.
Letters from French posts in the Gulf of Guinea, n.d.

1988–90. Dossier concerning the first Dahomey expedition.   **2005**
E.g., *1988.* Letters to Konakry, Cotonou, Porto Novo, Senegal containing much information about Dahomey, 1890–1.
1990. Letters from Senegal, St. Louis, etc., 1890–1.

1991. Minutes of the despatches from the commander of the French estab-   **2006**
lishments in Benin, etc., 1892–4.

1992. Letters received from the establishments at Benin, Porto Novo,   **2007**
1892–4.

2458. (d) Plan for exploring the Niger, 1889.   **2008**

2469. (h) Hydrographical expedition in Senegal, Niger, Congo, Lake   **2009**
Chad, 1906–13.

2528. (d) Correspondence about the above, 1910.   **2010**

4470. (g) Papers about the delimitation of French and Portuguese Guinea, **2011**
n.d.

LIBRARY OF THE MINISTRY OF MARINE
Bibliothèque de la Marine, 3 avenue Octave Gréard, Paris VIIe

The regulations for consultation are the same as those for the Service Historique,
see p. 89 above.

Catalogue of manuscripts: *Catalogue général des manuscrits des bibliothèques
publiques de France, Bibliothèque de la Marine,* by Ch. de la Roncière, Paris, 1907.

105. Atlas of maps and plans, manuscript and coloured, of Senegal and West
African coast, 1677–1822.

1. Map of African coasts, 1822.   **2012**

2. West African coast from Cape Blanc to R. Sierra Leone and R. Senegal   **2013**
and Gambia, Poirson, 1802.

3. Map of R. Senegal from mouth to Moussalla, Dupont, 1820.   **2014**

4. Map as above from Dagana to St. Louis, E. Bodin, 1821.   **2015**

5. Map of R. Senegal between Dagana and N. Guiau for land distribution,   **2016**
Courtois, 1820.

6. Map of islands of Thiong, Salsal and Yambord, north of St. Louis,   **2017**
Courtois, 1820.

7, 9. Map of mouth of R. Senegal and island of St. Louis, Courtois,   **2018**
1820.

10. Plan of English island in R. Senegal, Courtois, 1820.   **2019**

11. Map of south point of island of Babagué in mouth of R. Senegal,   **2020**
Courtois, n.d.

12. Plan of island of St. Louis, Courtois, 1820.   **2021**

13. Plan of fort in St. Louis, Courtois, 1820.   **2022**

Archives of the Congregation of the Fathers of the Holy Spirit

Congrégation des Pères du Saint-Esprit, 30 rue Lhomond, Paris Ve

The reading room is open from Monday to Saturday from 9 to 11.30 a.m., except during July and August.

The French missionary order of the Fathers of the Holy Spirit, or Spiritans, has been sending missionaries to West Africa since 1843. The archives of the order are conserved at the Mother House in Paris. They go back to the foundation of the order at the beginning of the eighteenth century, but great losses of eighteenth-century material occurred during the Revolution. The documents of the nineteenth and twentieth centuries are very numerous and important. The archives are extremely well kept. They are classified in a combined systematic and geographical order. The archivist, Father Bernard Noel, has prepared a typewritten inventory, which is nearly complete. As the archives are strictly private, the following conditions must be observed:

(1) The archives are the personal property of the Congregation of the Holy Spirit and cannot be consulted without the special permission of the Father General.

(2) The dossiers which can be consulted, i.e. dossiers of general and particular correspondence on the development and activities of the Congregation going back one hundred years are placed at the disposal of the historian on the undertaking, in writing, to publish nothing (articles, books) without the permission of the General Council of the Mother House.

The historian is allowed to microfilm with his own camera and on the spot the documents which he wants after he has made an explicit request to that effect and submitted to the archivist the documents he is interested in.

As the Spiritans have always been principally engaged in missionary work among the Negroes of Africa, their archives are clearly very important for the history of West Africa. The only printed guide is: *Notes et Documents relatifs à l'histoire de la Congrégation du Saint-Esprit sous la Garde de l'Immaculé Coeur de la B.V. Marie, 1703–1914*, Paris, 1917. This work is essentially a list of documents with a commentary. The main sets of documents are the series of letters and the series of journals kept by the communities of missionaries in Africa (*Journaux des communautés*). There are drawings, historical and linguistic notes, etc. The main items for West African history are the following.

CORRESPONDENCE

Boxes 81ff. Colonial clergy, colonial seminary, 1825–.   **2041**

Boxes 146–50. Various studies of the first missions, *inter alia*, in West Africa, **2042** including maps, linguistic notes, studies of the penetration of Islam amongst the negro population.

Boxes 152–64. Senegambia, from 1817.   **2043**

Boxes 165–70. Guinea, from 1803.   **2044**

Boxes 171–6. Gabon, from 1848.   **2045**

Boxes 183–90. Cameroon, from 1882.   **2046**

Boxes 191–2. Lower Niger, from 1884.   **2047**

Box 193. French Guinea, from 1876.   **2048**

Boxes 199–200. Sierra Leone, Gambia, Liberia, from 1850.   **2049**

JOURNALS OF THE MISSIONARY COMMUNITIES

No. 3. French Guinea (*boxes 674–5*): Boke, from 1896; Boffa, from 1875; **2050**
Sangha, from 1903.

No. 5. Libreville-Gabon (*boxes 677–81*): Cape Esterias, 1881; Bontika,   **2051**
from 1892; Apostolic Vicariate of Gabon, from 1897; Lambarence,
from 1880; Sainte-Croix des Eshiras, from 1895; Sainte-Anne du Fernan-
Vaz, from 1887; Saint-Michel de Ndjole, from 1897; Donguila, from
1887; Franceville, Saint-Hilaire, from 1897; Sindara, from 1899;
Libreville Mission Saint-Pierre, from 1884; District of Bangui: Saint-
Paul des Rapides, from 1894; Notre-Dame des Burse, from 1902; Sainte-
Famille de Ouadda, from 1894.

No. 7. Senegal (*boxes 671–3, 690*): Dakar, from 1874; Thies, from 1886;   **2052**
Rufisque, from 1860; Poponguine, from 1869; Ngasobil, from 1878; Joal,
from 1900; Fadiout, from 1887; Ziguinchor, from 1890; Carabane and
Sedhiou, from 1880; Thies, from 1903; Kaolack, from 1912; Poponguine,
from 1946; Fadiout, from 1921.

Father Sacleux C.S.Sp. (1856–1943) has left important notes and material for the
study of the popular language of the Comores, Swahili, and of the Bantu languages as well as maps, notes, and drawings relating to native art and folklore.
They are conserved among the Archives of the Congregation.

Paris Evangelical Missionary Society

Société des missions évangéliques de Paris, 102 Boulevard Arago, Paris XIVe

The archives are open from 9 a.m. to 12 and from 2 to 6 p.m. except during one
month in summer. Only documents from before 1900, in some cases 1914, may
be consulted. There is no catalogue or inventory.

According to a note kindly provided by the archivist most of the documents
of the Society concerning West Africa are not yet available as they only begin
in the twentieth century (Cameroon from 1917, and Togo from 1929 onwards).
Gabon, where the work of American missionaries was taken over in 1889 is
an exception. A few documents concern Senegal from 1862 onwards.

National Library

Bibliothèque Nationale, rue Richelieu, Paris IIe

The reading room is open to the public on presentation of a letter of introduction from the appropriate ambassador. The manuscript room is open every day

from 9 a.m. to 5 p.m. except for two weeks beginning on the Sunday after Easter.

There are many catalogues of these very large collections of manuscripts which are listed in: *Les catalogues imprimés de la Bibliothèque Nationale. Liste établie en 1943, suivie d'un supplément (1944–1952)*, Paris, 1953.

During the nineteenth century a catalogue according to the language of the manuscripts was begun—a system which is still followed—and some for smaller collections such as the *collection Colbert*. Manuscripts about West Africa are most likely to occur among *le Fonds français*. The catalogue of the basic collection is: *Catalogue des manuscrits français. Ancien fonds* (nos. 1–6170), 5 vols. Paris, 1868–1902. This was followed by a 13-volume supplement: *Catalogue général des manuscrits français*, by H. Omont, Paris, 1895–1918 (nos. 6171–33264 and new acquisitions nos. 1–11353 and 20001–22811).[1] There is a more recent *Catalogue général des manuscrits français. Table générale alphabétique des anciens et nouveaux fonds (nos. 1–33264) et des nouvelles acquisitions (nos. 1–10000)*, by A. Vidier and P. Perrier, 6 vols., Paris, 1931–48. Thus it is necessary to state when asking for a manuscript, whether it belongs to the *Ancien Fonds* or the *Nouvelles acquisitions*.[2] Further lists of acquisitions are published annually in the *Bibliothèque de l'Ecole des Chartes*. There is also a *Catalogue des manuscrits espagnols et des manuscrits portugais*, by A. Morelfatio, Paris, 1881–92.

In the reading room a *Catalogue alphabétique des livres imprimés mis à la disposition des lecteurs dans la salle de travail, suivi de la liste des catalogues usuels du Département des Manuscrits* is provided.

Fonds portugais

25. fo. 8. 89–91. Description of the Guinea Coast near St. George d'Elmina, seventeenth century (in Portuguese). **2053**

Fonds latin

Nouvelles acquisitions

n.a. 1112. Description (in Latin) of the basin of the Niger and Timbuctoo by Antonio Malfante, 1447.[3] **2054**

Fonds français

n.a. 6785. Collection of documents about the French colonies and the slave trade, 1797–1830. **2055**

n.a. 7485. fo. 87. Report by de Cussy on Senegal, 1685. **2056**

n.a. 9256–9510. Margry collection of copies of reports, letters, etc. in the archives of the Ministries of the Marine, Colonies etc., 256 volumes, various dates. **2057**

---

[1] The numbers 11354–20000 have not been used.
[2] In the following lists documents from the *Nouvelles acquisitions* are prefaced by the letters *n.a.* and from the original *Fonds français* by the letters F. fr.
[3] See Ch. de la Roncière, 'Découverte d'une relation de voyage datée du Touat et décrivant en 1447 le bassin du Niger', in the *Bulletin de la Section de Géographie*, Paris, 1918.

E.g., *9339*. Senegal. *fo. 6*. A copy of a pseudo-fourteenth-century description of the Guinea coast.

fo. 93. Report by Du Casse on the government of Arguin, 1678.

fo. 95. Copy of treaty with the Company of Senegal, 1769.

fo. 87. Copy of the sale of the privilege of the above company, 1681.

fo. 105. Copy of Du Casse's description of his travels in Guinea, 1687–8.

fo. 128. Journey by Damon in Guinea in 1698.

fo. 155. Report by Charpentier, the commander of the fort of St. Joseph in Galam, 1725.

9340. Senegal. *fo. 66*. Table of trade of the Compagnie des Indes, 1719–23.

fo. 111. Extracts from report by Pruneau de Pommegorge from Guinea and letter from Colombin of Nantes about his travels in Guinea, 1734.

fo. 121. Papers about Gabon.

9341. Compagnie des Indes. *fo. 41*. Instructions for Collé, commander of Galam, 1716.

fo. 64. Memorandum on Senegal.

fo. 115. Report on the river Falémé with plan by Duliron, 1747.

fo. 119. Letter from David, the governor of Senegal, 1740–5.

9353. Copies of documents about the Compagnie des Indes, 1664–1714.

9463. Log-books etc. about the campaigns in Casamance, 1841–2.

fo. 1. List of villages on banks of the river Casamance.

fo. 2. Copies of treaties with native chiefs in those parts e.g., at Itou, nineteenth century.

fo. 10. Report of commission sent to explore the bay of the coast including a detailed description of the coast between the rivers Gambia and Pongo and of the tribes inhabiting it and their agricultural methods, 1837.

fo. 29. Report on Sierra Leone, 1840–2.

fo. 35. Report from Goree, 1842.

fo. 56. Copy of a treaty between King Pepel of Bonny and the lieutenant of a French gunboat.

fo. 6off. Reports from Bonny, river Gabon, Accra, Axim, Whydah, 1842.

n.a. 10249. Papers about the hydrographical exploration of the Niger by Captain Lenfant, n.d.   **2058**

n.a. 10584. Report on West Africa by Dauriac and the places visited by the *Bellone*, 1867–9.   **2059**

n.a. 10726, 10727. Reports on Mizon's mission to the Niger and Benue, 1891–4.   **2060**

n.a. 11347. Travels on the coast and in the interior of West Africa, by Hecquart, 1850–1 (text different from that published in 1853).[1]   **2061**

n.a. 12240–74. Documents and correspondence about the companies of Africa, 1755.   **2062**

---

[1] H. Hecquart, *Voyage sur la côte et dans l'intérieur de l'Afrique occidentale*, Paris, 1853.

n.a. 12406–7. Collection of documents from the Chamber of Commerce **2063** of Normandy and the Seine-Maritime about the French colonies in Africa etc., 1771–1801.

n.a. 21393. Arnoul Collection. **2064**
E.g., *fo. 19.* Papers about the Guinea Company, 1685.
fo. 46. The Company's losses in Tacory, Kommenda etc., n.d.
fo. 59. Motives and ways of treating slaves, n.d.
fo. 63. Papers concerning the Portuguese methods of obtaining slaves, n.d.
fo. 71. Geographical details about the West African coast, Cape Blanc, island of Arguin, river Gambia, the Gold Coast, Cameroons, 1692.
fo. 79. Report on the Gold Coast, Senegal and Whydah, especially concerning trade, n.d.

n.a. 22085. fo. 409–35. Reports on Senegal, eighteenth and nineteenth centuries.

n.a. 22134–5. Collection of documents on the colonies and slavery. *I. fo.* **2065** *500.* Senegal, n.d.

n.a. 22186. Includes *fo. 249.* List of African ports, sixteenth century. **2066**

F. fr. 6244. fo. 40–184. 188–96. Two memoranda by M. Adanson on Gorée **2067** and French Guyane, 1760–9.[1]

F. fr. 6431. Report on the Compagnie royale d'Afrique, n.d. **2068**

F. fr. 9557. Collection, including *fo. 148.* Report on Senegal, 1760. **2069** *fo. 158.* Report on Bambouk, 1762.

F. fr. 11331. Extracts from the log-book of the *Sphère* on voyages to the **2070** West African coast in 1707–9.[2]

F. fr. 9669. fo. 8. Map of the West African coast made in Marseille in 1575. **2071**

F. fr. 12079. Report on Senegal and Goree, *inter alia*, rejecting English **2072** claims, *c.* 1755.

F. fr. 12080. Historical and political details of the religion, customs, and **2073** trade of the peoples of West Africa by Le Brasseur, 1778.

F. fr. 12395. Navigational instructions for, *inter alia*, the West African **2074** coast, n.d.

F. fr. 13057. Collection of manuscripts and pamphlets about the West **2075** African companies. Various dates.

F. fr. 15528. Collection de Harlay, including *fo. 524.* Papers about West **2076** African companies, 1683.

F. fr. 17309. fo. 92. Letter from the Hague concerning a 'monster' in Guinea, **2077** n.d.

F. fr. 20625. Narrative of the capture of the island of Goree, n.d. **2078**
F. fr. 21776–7. Nicolas Delamare Collection.

---

[1] See H. Froidevaux, *Les Mémoires d'Adanson*, Paris, 1899.
[2] See L. Baidaff, 'Extrait d'un journal de voyage fait en 1707, 1708 . . . aux côtes de Guinée en Afrique et à Buenos-Aires', in *Boletin de Instituto de Investigaciones historicas de Buenos Aires*, Ano VII, no. 40, 1929.

21776. Includes *fo. 156–8.* Report of the Company of Ostend, n.d.   **2079**

  fo. 239. Report on Guinea trade, n.d.   **2080**

21777. Includes *fo. 1–19.* Report on trade of Compagnie de Guinée, eighteenth century.   **2081**

F. fr. 24196. fo. 25. Description of Guinea, seventeenth century.   **2082**

F. fr. 24221–2. Descriptions of travels of de la Courbe in Africa and America (incomplete), 1685.[1]   **2083**

24222. fo. 306. Description of André Bruë's travels in Senegal, 1722–3.   **2084**

  fo. 365. Letter from Port Louis, 1724.   **2085**

  fo. 367. Letter from Captain Etienne La Rue on the capture of Fort Arguin from the Dutch, 1724.   **2086**

F. fr. 24223. Journal of Des Marchais in Guinea, giving information about native settlements and including sketches of the palace of Whydah, a map of the Kingdom of Whydah, sketches of natives, the coronation procession of the King of Whydah in 1725, sketches of native punishments, houses, utensils, weapons, 1724–6.   **2087**

F. fr. 24269, fo. 51. Remarks on the languages spoken in Guinea, sixteenth century.   **2088**

Colbert Collections

Collection des mélanges de Colbert.[2]

40. Copies of the charters of privileges granted by English kings to English companies, 1555–1670.   **2089**

135. fo. 38, 46. References to the capture of a Dutch vessel off the coast of West Africa, n.d.   **2090**

145. fo. 373. Report from d'Aliès on the voyage of a ship from Amsterdam to Guinea, 1667.   **2091**

147. fo. 96. Report to Colbert from Africa by Barthélémy de Groenenstein, for the King of Denmark and Norway, 1668.   **2092**

155. fo. 356. Report of a voyage by La Lande to Guinea, 1670.   **2093**

156. fo. 23–39. Description of a voyage by Captain d'Hailly on the *Tourbillon* to Rufisque, Kommenda, Elmina, Fort Nassau, difficulties with the Dutch, trade in ivory, seventeenth century.   **2094**

175. fo. 97. Request from merchants in West African trade for help against the Dutch, 1677.   **2095**

176. fo. 236. Report by d'Estrées on the trade of Cape Verde and Gambia, including map of the island of Goree, n.d.[3]   **2096**

Les Cinq Cents de Colbert.
Catalogue des manuscrits de la collection des Cinq Cents de Colbert, by Ch. de la Roncière, Paris, 1908.

[1] See J. Cultru, *Premier voyage du Sieur de la Courbe fait à la Coste d'Afrique en 1685,* Paris, 1913, being an edition of these manuscripts.
[2] *Catalogue des manuscrits de la collection des mélanges de Colbert,* by Ch. de La Roncière and P. M. Bondois, Paris, 1920.
[3] See A. Ly, *La compagnie du Sénégal de 1696 à 1673,* Bordeaux, 1955.

341. fo. 499 ff. Printed memoranda on quarrels in Guinea between the **2097**
Dutch and English, 1664 (in Dutch with French translation).

Maps and Plans

Cartes et plans

*Liste des cartes cédées à la Bibliothèque Nationale par le service central hydrographique
de la marine,* Portefeuilles 1–220, maps before 1800, which may be consulted in the
map room.

Portefeuille 109

1. Coast from Cape Blanc to Cape Negro, n.d.	**2098**
2. ,, ,, Sierra Leone, n.d.	**2099**
3. ,, of Guinea, n.d.	**2100**
4. A chart of the Guinea Coast, n.d.	**2101**
5. The coast from Sierra Leone to Cape of Good Hope, n.d.	**2102**
6. ,, Cape Blanc to the Cape of Good Hope, n.d.	**2103**
7. ,, Gallinas Point to Cape Lopez, 1714.	**2104**
7^1. ,, ,, ,,	**2105**
8. General map of the Guinea Coast, 1750.	**2106**
8^1. ,, ,, ,,	**2107**
9. ,, ,, ,,	**2108**
10. ,, West African coast, 1751.	**2109**
11. ,, ,, 1765.	**2110**
11^1. ,, ,, ,,	**2111**
12. Coast from Cape Blanc to Cape Lopez, 1765.	**2112**
13. ,, the Equator to 20° south, 1754.	**2113**
14. ,, Cape Frio to the Cape of Good Hope, 1754.	**2114**
15. ,, Cape Blanc ,, ,, n.d.	**2115**
15^1. ,, ,, ,, ,,	**2116**
16. ,, ,, ,, ,,	**2117**
17. ,, ,, Sierra Leone, n.d.	**2118**
18. Coast of Guinea, 1775.	**2119**
19. ,, from Sierra Leone to Cape Lopez, n.d.	**2120**
19^1. Coast from Sierra Leone to Cape Lopez, n.d.	**2121**
20. Coast from Cape Formosa to Sierra Leone, 1787.	**2122**
21. ,, ,, ,, 1791.	**2123**
22. ,, Lisbon to Sierra Leone, 1793.	**2124**
22^1. ,, ,, ,,	**2125**
23. ,, Cape Formosa to Cape Negro, 1794	**2126**

Portefeuille III

16/1.	W. African coast from Cape Blanc to Tombaly, 1736.		**2161**
17.	,,	Cape Blanc to mouth of R. Senegal, 1726.	**2162**
18.	,,	,, ,, n.d.	**2163**
19.	,,	Senegal to Cape Rouge, 1727.	**2164**
20.	,,	Cape Blanc to R. Gambia, n.d.	**2165**
20/1	,,	,, ,,	**2166**
21.	,,	,, Cape St. Mary, 1739.	**2167**
22.	,,	Cape Rouge to Cape Verga, n.d.	**2168**
23–23/3	,,	,, ,,	**2169**
24.	,,	Cape Blanc to the Gambia, n.d.	**2170**
24/1.	,,	,, ,,	**2171**
25.	,,	Cape Blanc to the Gambia, 1751.	**2172**
27.	,,	Cape Verde to the bank of St. Ann, 1752.	**2173**
28.	,,	Cape Blanc to Sierra Leone, n.d.	**2174**
30.	,,	,, Verga, n.d.	**2175**
31.	,,	,, Senegal, n.d.	**2176**
32.	,,	Cape Verde to Naze, n.d.	**2177**
33.	,,	Cape Blanc to R. Gambia, n.d.	**2178**
34.	,,	,, the bar of Senegal, 1776.	**2179**
37.	,,	Cape Verde to Verga, 1776.	**2180**
38.	,,	Rivers of Senegal, 1778.	**2181**
39.	,,	Senegal, 1780.	**2182**
40.	,,	Cape Blanc to R. Gambia, 1781.	**2183**
41.	,,	R. Saint-Jean to bar of Senegal, n.d.	**2184**
42.	,,	Goree to Sierra Leone, 1785.	**2185**
42/1.	,,	,, ,,	**2186**
43.	,,	Cape Verde to Cape St. Mary, 1785.	**2187**
44.	,,	Cape Mirick to Senegal, 1786.	**2188**
45.	,,	Senegal to the mouth of R. Gambia, 1786.	**2189**
46.	,,	R. Gambia, 1786.	**2190**
47.	,,	Senegal to R. Sherbro, 1787.	**2191**
48.	,,	Cape Blanc to entrance of R. Sierra Leone, 1788.	**2192**
49.	,,	Cape Blanc to Cape Verde, 1788.	**2193**
49/1–49/4	,,	,, ,,	**2194**
50.	,,	Countries adjoining the rivers Senegal and Gambia, n.d.	**2195**
52–52/1.	,,	Cape Blanc to the R. Gambia, n.d.	**2196**

Division 5

1. West African coast: Map of mouth of the R. Sherbro, n.d.					**2291**
2–2/2.	,,	,,	,,	1773.	**2292**
3.	,,	,,	R. Sierra Leone, n.d.		**2293**
4–4/2.	,,	,,	Entrance to Sierra Leone, n.d.		**2294**
5.	,,	,,	R. Sierra Leone, n.d.		**2295**
6.	,,	,,	Bay of Sierra Leone, n.d.		**2296**
7–11/1.	,,	,,	,, ,, and 1788, 1794.		**2297**

Division 6

1. West African coast: Map of R. Sestre, 1671.				**2298**
2–3/2.	,,	,,	River and village of Sestre, 1687.	**2299**
4–6.	,,		Cape Mesurado, n.d.	**2300**

Portefeuille 113

Division 1

2. West African coast: Map of castle of St. Anthony in Guinea, n.d.				**2301**
5.	,,	,,	Prince's island, n.d.	**2302**
6.	,,	,,	,,	**2303**
7.	,,	Sketches of the coast of Guinea, 1811.		**2304**

Portefeuille 7

41. West African coast: Plan of fort Amokou, n.d.				**2305**
42–42/1.	,,	Map of R. Banadari to St. Dominique, n.d.		**2306**
43.	,,	,,	harbour of Segou, n.d.	**2307**
44–44/1.	,,	,,	R. Benin, 1785.	**2308**
45.	,,	,,	little port of Elmina, n.d.	**2309**
46.	,,	,,	Shama, 1788.	**2310**
48.	,,	,,	Siram, n.d.	**2311**

Division 5

1. West African coast: Map of Gulf of Guinea, 1778.				**2312**
2.	,,	,,	Cape Formosa to island Corisco, n.d.	**2313**
3.	,,	,,	coast of Biafra, n.d.	**2314**
4.	,,	,,	Cape Formosa to Cape Lopez, n.d.	**2315**
5.	,,	,,	,, of Good Hope, 1787.	**2316**
6.	,,	,,	Cape St. Jean to Cape Padron, n.d.	**2317**
7.	,,	,,	R. San Benito to Cape Three Points, 1793.	**2318**
7/1.	,,	,,	R. San Benito ,, n.d.	**2319**
8.	,,	,,	Cape Formosa to Cape Negro, 1794.	**2320**
8/1.	,,	,,	Cape Ste. Cathérine to Cape Verde, n.d.	**2321**

9. West African coast: Map of Cape Formosa to Foko, 1795.   **2322**

31.   ,,   ,,   R. Calabar, n.d.   **2323**

32.   ,,   Plan of R. Bonny and New Calabar, 1699.   **2324**

33.   ,,   ,,   ,,   1778.   **2325**

34.   ,,   ,,   ,,   1785.   **2326**

Division 6
1–2/1. West African coast: Map of Fernando Po, n.d.   **2327**

3.   ,,   ,,   harbour of St. Charles, n.d.   **2328**

Portefeuille 8

Division 7
1–1/1. West African coast: Map of Prince's island and St. Thomas island, **2329**
                n.d.

2–2/1.   ,,   ,,   Port of St. Anthony, n.d.   **2330**

3–5.   ,,   ,,   Prince's island, 1778, 1779.   **2331**

6–6/1.   ,,   ,,   Port of Prince's island, n.d.   **2332**

7–8/4.   ,,   ,,   ,,   **2333**

Division 8
1. West African coast: Plan of fort of St. Sebastian, n.d.   **2334**

2.   ,,   ,,   St. Thomas' island, n.d.   **2335**

2/1–4.   ,,   ,,   ,,   ,,   **2336**

Portefeuille 114

Division 1
1. West African coast: Map of Anamabou, n.d.   **2337**

2.   ,,   ,,   View of Prince's island, n.d.   **2338**

Portefeuille 120

Division 2
75/1–82. West African coast: Map of Cape Verde island, n.d., 1775, 1794. **2339**

Division 7
1–13. West African coast: Map of Cape Verde islands and ports therein,   **2340**
n.d. or eighteenth century.

MAIN MAP AND PLAN ARCHIVES
Grandes archives

Catalogue des portulans du Service hydrographique de la Marine, by Georges Deulin,
1942 (typed).

no. 1. Marine map of the world, including the West African coast and the **2341**
site of Elmina, by Nicolas de Canerio, n.d.
Service hydrographique de la Marine: Archive no. 3.[1]

[1] The order of the catalogue has been followed in this list.

Planisphere showing Angola, and a sketch of the castle of Elmina, by **2342**
Domingos Teixira, n.d.

no. 18. General map of the West African coast, decorated by a sketch of **2343**
Elmina castle, by J. Teixeira Albernas, 1667.

no. 38. Marine map of the world with a view between Guinea and Ethiopia, **2344**
by P. de Lemos, end sixteenth century.

no. 13. Marine map of Guinea, Brazil etc., by J. Aertsz. Colon, printed, **2345**
1631.

no. 36. Map of the West Indies including the Guinea coast, by H. Doucker, **2346**
printed, n.d.

no. 20. Same by P. Goos, printed, 1666. **2347**

no. 14. Plan showing, *inter alia*, Cape Verde, R. Volta, Angola, R. Gambia, **2348**
Senegal and the Niger by Jean Guerard, 1631.

no. 15. Universal map including Cape Verde, Guinea, Senegal and Niger, **2349**
by Jean Guerard, n.d.

no. 9. Coasts of America and those of Africa including Cape Lopez and **2350**
Elmina, by Jean Dupont, 1625.

no. 6. Marine map of the west coasts of Europe, Africa including Benin, **2351**
Elmina, Cape Verde, by Pierre de Vaulx, 1613.

Marine maps (*portulans*)

Répertoire des portulans et des cartes sur vélin, by M. G. Deulin, 1935 (typed).

13. (Réserve Ge. *DD 1988*). Five-page atlas including the West African **2352**
coast, by G. Benincasa, 1467.

19. (Réserve Ge. *B. 1132*). Marine map including the West African coast, **2353**
by G. Viegas, 1534.

21. (Réserve Ge. *C. 5097*). Same, attributed to Viegas, n.d. **2354**

28. (Réserve Ge. *B. 1204*). Marine map including the greater part of **2355**
Africa, anon., n.d.

32. (Réserve Ge. *CC. 2719*) *fo. 3.* Atlantic, Europe, and West Africa, by **2356**
A. Homem, 1659.

42. (Réserve Ge. *DD. 682*) Atlas *fo. 5.* Africa, by J. Martines, 1583. **2357**

44. Marine map including the African coast including Gambia, by M. **2358**
Prunes, 1586.

53. (Réserve Ge. *FF. 14409*) Atlas *fo. 9.* West Africa, anon. Portuguese, **2359**
end sixteenth–early seventeenth century.

70. Marine map of African coasts, by D. Sanches, 1618. **2360**

77. Map of West Africa, by S. Oliva, 1630. **2361**

90. as *no. 20*, by P. Goos, above. **2362**

93. Map of the West African coast as far as Arguin, by Roussin, n.d. **2363**

102. Same, anon., n.d. **2364**

5. Marine map of the Atlantic including the West African coast north of **2365**
Biafra, by G. Levasseur, 1601.

19. Map including Guinea, by Du Bocage Boissaye, 1669.   **2366**

22. Map of the coasts of Europe, West Africa etc. including Prince's Island, **2367**
St. Thomas, Guinea, Sierra Leone, Cape Palmas, by Debeaulieu, 1672.

34. Map of the coasts of Africa, the Grain Coast, Guinea etc., anon., n.d. **2368**

35. Map of the coast from Cape Palmas to the Cape of Good Hope, anon., **2369**
n.d.

37. Map of the African and European coasts including Cape Palmas, anon., **2370**
n.d.

D'Anville Collection

Catalogue géographique; collection D'Anville: Asie, Océanie, Afrique.

8083. Africa . . . the country of negroes, Guinea and neighbouring coun- **2371**
tries, by Sansom, 1655.

8084. Map of the African coast from Cape Verde to the island of St. **2372**
Thomas, by Sanuto, n.d.

8085. Map of Nigritte and Guinea, by P. du Val, 1653.   **2373**

8086. Guinea and Ethiopia by D'Anville, 1743.   **2374**

8087. Map of the African coast including part of Guinea, the Kingdom of **2375**
Benin, St. Thomas' Island, anon., n.d.

8088. Map of the West African coast as far as Cape Verde, by Sanuto, n.d. **2376**

8090. Map of the African coasts including the Kingdom of Gualata etc. for **2377**
the King of Portugal, by Mortier, n.d.

8091. Coast of Gualata, Dutch, 1684.   **2378**

8092. Map of the African coast from Cape Blanc to the Gold Coast, by **2379**
D'Anville, n.d.

8093. Same, from Whydah to Baxal point, by D'Anville, n.d.   **2380**

General maps of the country watered by the R. Senegal

8095. Map of French Africa, or Senegal etc., by Delisle, 1726.   **2381**

8096. Map of West Africa between Arguin and Sierra Leone etc., by **2382**
D'Anville, 1727.

8097. English map of the West African coast from Cape Blanc to Cape **2383**
Verga, by Jefferys, n.d.

8098. Map of the West African coast from Cape Blanc to Cape Verga, by **2384**
D'Anville, 1791.

8099. Map of the West African coast from Cape Blanc to R. Sierra Leone, **2385**
by de la Courbe, n.d.

8100. English map of West African coast from Cape Blanc to R. Sierra **2386**
Leone, by Lewis Sorel and Thomas Walker, n.d.

8101. Map of the West African coast from Cape Blanc to Cape Verga, by **2387**
D'Anville, n.d.

8102. Dutch map of the West African coast from Cape Blanc to the Rio **2388**
Grande, by Henry Doucker, n.d.

8103. Map of the coast of Senegal from Cape Blanc to the R. Gambia, **2389**
anon., n.d.

8104. Same, anon., 1769. **2390**

Details of the West African coast from Cape Blanc to Senegal

8105. MS. map of the coast of Portendic to the bar of Senegal, n.d. **2391**

8106. MS. map from 19° 30″ N. to Cape Blanc, n.d.[1] **2392**

8107. Dutch map of the coast round Arguin, by J. Robyn, 1684. **2393**

8108. MS. map as above by D'Anville, n.d. **2394**

8109. Map of coast between Cape Blanc and R. Saint Jean, anon., n.d. **2395**

8110. Map from Cape Blanc to Tanit, anon., n.d. **2396**

8111 and *8112*. Plans of Bay and island of Arguin, anon., n.d. **2397**

8113. Fort Arguin by Compagnon, 1716. **2398**

8114.   ,,   Périer de Salvert, 1721. **2399**

8115. Plan of Portendic by Labat, n.d. **2400**

8116. Map of Bay of Portendic, anon., n.d. **2401**

Details of R. Senegal

8117. MS. map of the coast near Goree and R. Senegal from Cagneux to **2402**
mouth, by D'Anville, 1724.

8118. Same, of R. Senegal. **2403**

8119. MS. map of R. Senegal, by Bruë's orders, 1720. **2404**

8120. Course of R. Senegal, to Desere, anon., n.d. **2405**

8121, 8122, and *8123.* Mouth of R. Senegal, to Desere, anon., n.d. **2406**

8124. Plan of island of Senegal, anon., 1745. **2407**

8125. Island of St. Louis and R. Senegal, anon., n.d. **2408**

8126, 8127, and *8128.* MS. plans of Fort St. Louis on island of Senegal, **2409**
anon., n.d.

8129. MS. map of R. Senegal from Oualade to Dolole by D'Anville, n.d. **2410**

8130. Same, from Dolole to Louton, n.d. **2411**

8131. Map of R. Falémé, anon., 1716. **2412**

8132. Fort of St. Joseph in Galam, by Labat, n.d. **2413**

8133. Second arm of R. Senegal unknown up to now, anon., n.d. **2414**

8134. Plan of Félou hills, anon., n.d. **2415**

8136. Map of the Province of Gelofo and the kingdom of Cacheo, anon., **2416**
n.d.

8137. Same, from Cape Verde to Sherbro, n.d. **2417**

8138. MS. map from Cape Verde and Sauvages Island to Cape Taguin, by **2418**
de la Courbe, n.d.

[1] These are two parts of one map.

8139. Same, from Cape Verde to Cape Verga, n.d.   **2419**

8140. MS. map of the concession of company of Senegal from Cape Blanc **2420**
to Bissau, anon., n.d.

8141. MS. from bar of Senegal to R. St. Dominique with the course of **2421**
the R. Gambia, anon., n.d.

8142. Same, coast of Cape Verde, n.d.   **2422**

8143, and *8145*. Plans of island of Goree, anon., n.d.   **2423**

8144. Plan of Island of Goree, anon., 1677.   **2424**

8146 and *8147*. Plans of island of Goree, with fortifications, anon., n.d. **2425**

8148. Views of Cape Verde and island of Goree, anon., n.d.   **2426**

8149. MS. of R. Gambia from mouth to Kingdom of Ouly.   **2427**

8150. R. Gambia to Eropina, by Jean Leach, 1732.   **2428**

8151. R. Gambia from Eropina to Barra Konda, 1732.   **2429**

8152. R. Gambia to Eropina, 1732.   **2430**

8153. R. Gambia from Eropina to Barra Konda, anon., n.d.   **2431**

8154. R. Gambia and surroundings, n.d.   **2432**

8155. Mouth of R. Gambia, by D'Anville, n.d.   **2433**

8156 and *8157*. MS. plans of Fort Jacques on R. Gambia, anon., n.d.   **2434**

8158. Coast between Cape Rouge and R. Nuñez, anon., n.d.   **2435**

8161. Same, from Cape Verde to Cape of Good Hope, anon., n.d.   **2436**

8162. Same, of Guinea coast to Cape of Good Hope, anon., n.d.   **2437**

8163. Map of Guinea: Nova Descriptio, anon., n.d.   **2438**

8164. Map of Guinea coasts with the Kingdoms known to Europeans, **2439**
anon., 1677.

8165. Map of Guinea, anon., n.d.   **2440**

8171. West African coast including part of Guinea and Elmina, anon., n.d. **2441**

8172. Dutch map of Guinea coast to Cape Palmas, anon., n.d.   **2442**

8173 and *8174*. Guinea coast from R. Sierra Leone to Cape Valmar, anon., **2443**
1746.

8175. Coast and countries beside R. Sierra Leone and Sherbro, anon., n.d. **2444**

8176 and *8177*. Mouth of R. Sierra Leone and Sherbro, anon., n.d.   **2445**

8178. Bay of Sierra Leone and view of entrance, anon., n.d.   **2446**

8179. Mouth of Sherbro, anon., n.d.   **2447**

8180. Guinea coast from Cape Monte to Bassam, anon., n.d.   **2448**

8181. Two views of Cape Monte, anon., n.d.   **2449**

8182, *8183*, and *8184*. Cape Mesurado and entrance to river, anon., n.d. **2450**

8185. Native houses of Cape Mesurado, anon., n.d.   **2451**

8186, *8187*, and *8188*. Mouth of R. Sestro, anon., n.d.   **2452**

8231. View of English fort at Whydah, anon., n.d.   **2488**

8232. Palace of King Xavier of Whydah by Des Marais, n.d.   **2489**

8233. View of European trading posts at Xavier, anon., n.d.   **2490**

8234. View of Whydah, anon, n.d.   **2491**

8235. Drawings of coronation procession, anon., n.d.   **2492**

8236. Drawings of torture of man and woman caught in adultery in Why-   **2493**
dah, anon., 1725.

8237–41. Sketches of the natural objects of Whydah, anon., n.d.   **2494**

8242. Map of Gulf of Guinea, anon., n.d.   **2495**

8243 and *8244*. Maps of R. Calabar anon., 1699.   **2496**

Library of the Institut de France

Bibliothèque de l'Institut, 23 quai Conti, Paris VIe

Readers must be introduced by two members of the *Institut*. The library is closed from July 15 to September 30.

Catalogue général des manuscrits des bibliothèques publiques de France, Bibliothèque de l'Institut, Ancien et nouveau fonds, Paris, 1928, and *Collection Godefroy*, Paris, 1914.

ANCIEN ET NOUVEAU FONDS

1067–1218. Notes by Charles-Joseph de Pougens, *inter alia* cxx (1186) on   **2497**
the polyglotic philology of West Africa, 1755–1833.

488. Mélanges historiques, Recueil B.

fo. 451. Copy of letters from Plumet, the director of Fort St. Joseph in   **2498**
Galam, to the directors of the Company, 1728.

fo. 469, 475. Extracts from letters about the gold mines of Galam and   **2499**
Bambouk, n.d.

COLLECTION GODEFROY

516. Recueil. fo. 443. Plan for a fort on the African coast, n.d.   **2500**

68. Copies of papers about trade and navigation, 1484 to seventeenth   **2501**
century. E.g., *fo. 9*, remarks on the Gold Coast, n.d.

Library of Sainte-Geneviève

Bibliothèque Sainte-Geneviève, place du Panthéon, Paris Ve

The manuscripts are kept in the *Réserve*, which is open every day from 10 a.m. to midday, and from 2 until 6 p.m. A reader's ticket, bearing a passport photograph, must be obtained, or a reader's ticket of the *Bibliothèque Nationale* shown.

See the *Catalogue des manuscrits de la bibliothèque Sainte-Geneviève*, 3 vols., Paris, 1893–8.

529. Description of the geography of the coasts of France . . . West Africa **2502** . . . etc., with notes by P. Pingré, eighteenth century.

1813. fo. 1. Sketch of the trade of West Africa, between Gallinas and Gabon **2503** by E. Bouët, Commander of the *Malouine*, 1838–9 (copy). *fo. 79.* Same, by Captain Broquant, 1838–9 (copy).

1823. Various geographical notes, including *fo. 7.* List of animal products **2504** of Goree and the Cape Verde Islands, *fo. 30.* Note on the mulattoes of Goree and the native traders in the town, eighteenth century.

1824. Copy of description of the character of the Arabs living between **2505** Mount Atlas and the River Senegal by the English captain, John Glass, eighteenth century.

3002. Treatise on geography containing, *inter alia*, a few remarks on **2506** West Africa, seventeenth century.

PART II

ARCHIVES AND LIBRARIES
OUTSIDE PARIS

Aix-en-Provence

MÉJANES LIBRARY

Bibiothèque Méjanes, Hôtel de Ville, Aix-en-Provence

The reading room is opened on request.

Catalogue général des manuscrits des bibliothèques publiques de France, vol. XVI, Paris, 1894.

232 (759–R 10). Description of a voyage to Guinea and the American **2507** islands by François de Paris, with map, seventeenth century.

233 (431–R 167). Description of a voyage to island of St. Thomas, by **2508** Bailly, with map, 1708–9.

Amiens

DEPARTMENTAL ARCHIVES

Archives départementales de la Somme, 88bis rue Gaulthier-de-Rumilly, Amiens

The reading room is open from Monday to Friday from 9 a.m. to midday, and 2 p.m. to 5 p.m. and on Saturdays from 9 a.m. to 12, except from July 1 to 15.

The documents of the *Intendance de Picardie*, which contain, *inter alia*, the archives of the Chamber of Commerce before 1790, are inventoried by G. Durand, *Inventaire sommaire des archives départementales antérieures à 1790, vol. II–IV: Intendance*, Amiens, 1888–97.

C 410. Permission of the Conseil d'Etat to merchants from Picardy to **2509** trade in Guinea, printed, 1754.

Arras

Town Library

Bibliothèque municipale d'Arras, Palais Saint-Vaast, rue Paul-Doumer, Arras

Manuscripts listed in the *Catalogue général des manuscrits des bibliothèques publiques de France*, vol. XL, *Supplément*, Paris, 1902. Arras manuscripts *1129, 1130* have been destroyed.

Besançon

Town Library

Bibliothèque municipale, Besançon, Doubs

The reading room is open every day from 9.30 a.m. to midday and from 1.30 to 6 p.m., except for two weeks at Easter and July 1–15.

Catalogue général des manuscrits des bibliothèques publiques de France, vol. XXXII, Paris, 1897, and *Supplément*, vol. XLV, Paris, 1915.

888. Description of the journey from Senegal to Galam by land, by **2510** Durand, 1786.

Bordeaux

I. Departmental Archives

Archives départementales de la Gironde, 13–25 rue d'Aviau, Bordeaux

The reading room is open every day from 8.30 a.m. to 12 and from 2 to 6.30 p.m., and on Saturdays from 8.30 a.m. to 12, except from July 1 to 15.

Among the main series are the archives of the chamber of commerce (registers of Series C, no. 4250–439) with eighteenth century material. The more recent archives of the Chamber of Commerce were lost in 1940; the archives of the port were burnt in 1919. The series Admiralty (6 B) and Consular Jurisdiction (7 B) are also of interest.[1]

[1] See introductory note to the section of the Archives of the Ministry of Marine, p. 89.

Series B. *Amirauté de Guienne et Juridiction consulaire*

M. Oudot de Dainville, *Archives départementales de la Gironde, Répertoire numérique des fonds de l'Amirauté de Guienne et de la Juridiction consulaire*, Bordeaux, 1913. The documents in the archives of the Admiralty belong to the period 1640–1792. There are documents on the slave trade and on the voyages of Bordeaux ships generally, while the registers of the Consular Jurisdiction contain information on trade.

The *Répertoire numérique* is extremely summary and gives little more than numbers and dates of documents with the briefest indication of their contents. A typewritten alphabetical index of persons' names exists for the numbers *6B22–6B38: Registres de réceptions de capitaines de navires, chirurgiens, maîtres de barque*, etc. *1699–1792, Table alphabétique des noms*.

In the Series 7B, Consular Jurisdiction, there is an important section concerning bankrupt commercial firms, whose account books and other papers may be useful for the study of French trade in Africa in the eighteenth century. There is a brief survey: F. Giteau, *Archives Départementales de la Gironde, Répertoire numérique du Fonds des Négociants (7B 1001 à 3154)*, Bordeaux, 1960. This series contains documents from some 650 firms and the virtually complete archives of 41 firms. The following are important items:

7B 1982. Dossier of documents on the slave trade, concerning the *François*, 1763. **2511**

7B 3041. Collection of miscellaneous documents concerning the slave trade, 1748–86. **2512**

Series C. *Chambre de Commerce*

J. A. Brutails, *Inventaire sommaire des archives départementales antérieures à 1790, Gironde, Série C, III, mss. 4250–439, Chambre de Commerce de Guienne*, Bordeaux, 1893, vol. IV (contains an alphabetical index for the whole Series C). J. A. Brutails and G. Loirette, *Inventaire sommaire des archives départementales antérieures à 1790, Gironde, Archives Civiles, Série C, t. IV*, pp. 113–396.[1]

C. 4257, fo. 252–252 vo. Letter from the Minister of the Marine, de Sartine, about a premium of £15 per negro bought on the African coast and transported to the French colonies in the West Indies. The letter refers particularly to the case of one Mr. Dudemaine Quimper, captain of a vessel from Bordeaux, who had bought 194 negroes, 27 February 1777. **2513**

C. 4258. **2514**
E.g., *fo. 182*. References to a request for the monopoly of the gum trade instead of a monopoly of the slave trade from Cape Verde to the river of Casamance, 29 January 1784.

fo. 244. References to a temporary monopoly of the slave trade from the left bank of the river Formosa; offers to build a fortress by Brillantois, Marion & Co., 6 July 1786.

fo. 276 vo. Letter from Marshal de Castries about the amenability of the negroes of Cape Laho, promising traders the protection of the royal navy against the traders of other nations, 12 July 1787.

[1] This series has been extensively used by S. Berbain, *Le comptoir français de Juda (Ouidah) au XVIIIe siècle. Etude sur la traite des noirs au golfe de Guinée*, Mémorandum de l'Institut français d'Afrique noire, no. 3, Paris, 1942.

C. 4251. **2515**

E.g., *fo. 12.* Letter from the Directors of Commerce of La Rochelle to Bordeaux about events on the Gold Coast, 10 April 1788.

fo. 20 vo. Letter from Count de la Luzerne about the slave trade at Porto Novo and Badagry on the Gold Coast, suggesting that these places are better than Whydah where trade is slack, 13 November 1788.

fo. 48 vo. Letters concerning the freeing of negro slaves, 21 January 1790.

fo. 67. Letter addressed to traders and captains of Bordeaux by the king of Ardres on the Guinea Coast about certain rules imposed on traders: import quotas are imposed on certain goods. The letter is dated 4 November 1790, 24 March 1791.

C. 4262. **2516**

E.g., *fo. 206 vo.* Letter about the English slave traders at Anamabou, 23 September 1738.

fo. 201 vo. Letter about English forts on the Anamabou coast, 9 December 1738.

fo. 210. English fort at Anamabou; short history of the fort since 1665, 30 December 1738.

C. 4263. **2517**

E.g., *fo. 118 vo.* Letter to Minister of the Marine about the hostility of the English on the Guinea coast, 20 December 1749.

fo. 138 vo–139. A French boat having stopped at Cape Casse(?) on the Guinea coast the English governor of the fort there tells the captain that he can provide him with negroes as cheaply as in Anamabou. Some historical information about the slave trade, 27 February 1751.

C. 4265. **2518**

E.g., *fo. 56–56 vo.* Letter about the trade from Captain Quimper, mentioning Malymbe, 12 April 1777.

C. 4266. **2519**

E.g., *fo. 17–17 vo.* Letter to Marshal de Castries about the explorations by the Marquess de la Jaille relating to trade on the Gambia. Frontiers with Portuguese territory in the direction of Cape Monte, 26 July 1785.

fo. 46 vo. Letter to the Directors of Commerce of Nantes, La Rochelle and St. Malo about the slave markets of Ouerre and Benin and on the estuary of the Formosa river. Construction of a fort, information about the coast. Monopoly of the slave trade by Brillantois, Marion and Company of St. Malo, 8 July 1786.

fo. 215 vo. Letter to the Minister of the Marine about the port of Ambris on the coast of Angola. Safety of trade, 6 December 1791.

C. 4270. **2520**

E.g., *fo. 138–40.* Information about the slave trade at Whydah and the situation of the port, 27 January 1724.

C. 4271. **2521**

E.g., *fo. 130 vo–131 vo.* Mention of the attack of King Dahomet (*sic*) on Whydah, where French boats had gone to trade; the king of Whydah taken prisoner, 22 August 1727.

The Parlement of Bordeaux

This institution, from the fifteenth century onwards played an important part not only in the administration of the law but also in all matters of government.

J. A. Brutails, *Inventaire sommaire des archives départementales antérieures à 1790, Gironde, Série B—Archives Judiciaires. Registres d'enregistrement du Parlement, 1 B1 à 58.* Bordeaux, 1925, index by G. Loirette. There are also three typewritten lists, namely: *Arrêts du Parlement de Bordeaux 1463–1666, Répertoire*—a mere list of numbers and dates; *Arrêts du Parlement de Bordeaux, Table des noms de lieux et de matières*, and *Catalogue (chronologique) des arrêts de portée générale du Parlement de Bordeaux, Supplément, 1700–90*, with a *Table alphabétique*.

E.g., *arrêt* of 1 August 1679 concerning the Compagnie de Sénégal and   **2527** its trade on the Coast of Africa from Cape Verde to the Cape of Good Hope. There are also *arrêts* concerning coloured people and the slave trade of 21 November 1716, 14 December 1716, 17 February 1739, 19 January 1717, and 4 February 1778.

Notarial Papers

This voluminous series goes back to the late Middle Ages and contains the record of all sorts of transactions before notaries of the Bordeaux region. They include, *inter alia*, commercial contracts relating to trade overseas. The use of this mass of documents is very difficult because of the lack of adequate inventories and indexes. For Series E, see G. Chauvet and J. Barennes, *Archives départementales de la Gironde, Répertoire numérique notarial et terriers de la garde-note (3 E)*, Bordeaux, 1913—a purely numerical list. More information can be found in the typewritten sixteen-volume list of notaries, with numbers and dates of their dossiers, which can be consulted in the reading room. There is, however, no indication about the contents of these notarial papers. There exists an old alphabetical list of notaries of the *Ancien Régime*: M. Faugas, *Catalogue des notaires dont les pratiques sont à la Garde-Note*, Bordeaux, 1762.

E.g., *3 E 2965.* Commercial contract concluded before the notary   **2528** J. Castaigne between Martin de Malus, master of the Mint of Bordeaux

---

[1] This and the following items are dossiers of documents received instead of registers with copies.

and Jean de Martineau, who accompanies Captain Peyrot de Monluc to Benin; trade and transport of goods, division of the profits, 21 August 1566.

Series J. Families

The papers of a certain number of families of the Bordeaux region are assembled here. There are fewer commercial papers than one would expect; many more are probably still in private hands and are difficult to consult. There are some interesting collections of scholars' notes.

Fv. Giteau, *Archives départementales de la Gironde, Dons et Acquisitions, Répertoire de la série J, Fonds principaux*, Bordeaux, 1955. This deals with 5 J–10 J, and analyses the documents family by family. There is an alphabetical index of persons and places at the end. For 1 J–4 J, see the manuscript survey: *Répertoire des Séries 1 J, 3 J, 4 J*.

E.g., *3 J/C 11*, Le Tellier. Copy of letters of Messrs. Forcade, slavers   **2529** of Bordeaux, concerning the sale of 263 negroes of the *Bonne Henriette*, 1791.

8 J 422, Bigot. Small dossier concerning the slave trade; company   **2530** formed in Dunkirk for the equipment of the frigate *Le Dauphin* for the Guinea trade. Data on various voyages, e.g. of the *Comte d'Artois* with 240 negroes on board, 1774–8.

Maps and Plans (*Cartes et Plans*)

II 2 1582bis. Portulan of the late fifteenth century showing the west coast   **2531** of Africa as far as the Rio do Padrom, i.e., the Congo estuary. This parchment portulan, signed Pedro Renel, measures *c.* 1 metre by 1.5 metre and is a very early and important document. It is to be published in vol. V of the *Portugaliae Monumenta Cartographica*.

II. TOWN LIBRARY
3 rue Mably, Bordeaux

The reading room is open every day from 9 a.m. to 12 and from 2 to 7 p.m. C. Couderc, *Catalogue des manuscrits de la bibliothèque de Bordeaux*, Paris, 1894 (*Catalogue général des manuscrits*). First supplement: *Catalogue général des manuscrits des bibliothèques publiques de France*, vol. XL, *Supplément I*, Paris, 1902. Second supplement: *Catalogue général des manuscrits des bibliothèques publiques de France*, vol. L, *Départements*, Paris, 1954.

715. Geographical treatise dealing with Africa, eighteenth century.   **2532**

1570. Register of the commercial shipping of Bordeaux, 1791–3.   **2533**

1582. Same, 1792–3.   **2534**

Caen

DEPARTMENTAL ARCHIVES

Archives départementales de Calvados, 1 Parvis Notre-Dame, Caen

The reading room is open from Monday to Friday from 9 a.m. to midday, and from 2 to 6 p.m. and on Saturdays from 9 a.m. to midday, except from July 1 to 15.

The archives of the Chamber of Commerce have been entirely destroyed. As well as the departmental archives which contain nothing of much importance for West Africa, the same building has housed the manuscript collection of the Public Library since its own building was destroyed. See the *Catalogue général des manuscrits des bibliothèques publiques de France, Départements,* XIV (1890) 215–380: *Caen,* by G. Lavalley. *Suppléments* in vols. XLI (1903) and XLIV (1911) 1–310 *Collection Mancel,* by R.-N. Sauvage.

562(281–*in folio 177*). *Papers of General Decaen:*   **2535**
E.g., 95. Includes historical notes on Senegal by du Bocage with map. Geographical and political analyses of Arguin, Portendic and the gum trade. Native villages. The island of St. Louis. The Trarzas of the River Senegal—their weapons etc. The islands in the mouth of the Senegal. Lake Cayor. King of Brac and his rights, powers, and army. King Damel of Cayor. The climate of Goree. The Kingdom of Bar. English forts and possessions; followed by suggestions for improving the colony, 1788.

2. Copy of printed memorandum on Africa by Jerôme Lalande, Paris, *An* **2536** III.

3. Reflections on the destruction of Fort James, incomplete, n.d.   **2537**

Calais

TOWN LIBRARY

Bibliothèque municipale, 1 rue de Vic, Calais

The reading room is open every day from 8 a.m. to 12 and from 2 to 6 p.m. except Friday afternoon, and the month of August.

Catalogue général des manuscrits des bibliothèques publiques de France, LXI, Paris, 1903.

88. Report on the wreck of the *Méduse* by G. Mollien, which describes,   **2538**
inter alia, excursions near Rufisque (p. 39); a voyage from St. Louis to
Podor (p. 54); and remarks on the natives of Senegambia, 1822.

94. Description of a voyage to China by G. Mollien with, *inter alia*, some   **2539**
notes on Africa (*fo. 243*), 1853.

Carpentras

INGUIMBERTINE LIBRARY

Bibliothèque Inguimbertine, Carpentras, Vaucluse

The reading room is open every day from 10 a.m. to 12, and from 2 to 7 p.m.
except Wednesdays, and the month of August.

Catalogue général des manuscrits des bibliothèques publiques de France, vols.
XXXIV, XXXV, XXXVI, Paris, 1901–3.

1864. Collection including, *inter alia*, description of African natives and   **2540**
their origins, character, and relations with Europeans, seventeenth
century.

1777. Collection including a description of the Guinea coast, n.d.   **2541**

Clermont-Ferrand

DEPARTMENTAL ARCHIVES

Archives départementales du Puy-de-Dôme, Préfecture, Clermont-Ferrand

The reading room is open every day from 9.30 a.m. to 12 and from 2 to 6 p.m.
and on Saturdays from 9.30 a.m. to 12.

There is an *Inventaire Sommaire de la série C*, vol. I by M. Cohendy, Clermont-
Ferrand, 1893, and vols. II–VI by G. Rouchon, 1898–1916, and a *Table alphabétique générale* of vols. I–IV by G. Rouchon, 1937.

1 C 808–15. Papers of the Compagnie des Indes concerning trade with,   **2542**
inter alia, West Africa, n.d.

Dinan

TOWN LIBRARY

Bibliothèque municipale, Dinan, Côtes-du-Nord

The reading room is open every day from 8.45 a.m. to 12 and from 2 to 6.45 p.m., except Monday morning, Wednesday afternoon, and the month of August.

Catalogue général des manuscrits des bibliothèques publiques de France, vol. XLI, Paris, 1903.

6. Portuguese map, including Africa, 1632. **2543**

Dunkirk

CHAMBER OF COMMERCE

Chambre de commerce et d'industrie de Dunkerque, 1 Quai Freyernet, Dunkerque

Documents may be consulted on application every working day between 8.30 a.m. and midday, and from 2 to 6 p.m., and on Saturday from 8.30 a.m. to midday.

Information about West Africa may be sought in the *délibérations*, and *déclarations des Capitaines*, but there is no inventory.[1]

Epernay

TOWN LIBRARY

Bibliothèque de la ville d'Epernay, 13 avenue de Champagne, Epernay, Marne

The reading room is open every day except Sunday and Tuesday, holidays and the month of August, from 1.30 to 6 p.m.

[1] See L. Lemaire, 'Dunkerque et la Traite des noirs au 18e siècle', in the *Bulletin de l'Union Faulconnier*, vol. XXXI, Dunkirk, 1934.

Catalogue général des manuscrits des bibliothèques publiques de France, vol. XXIV, Paris, 1894.

151. Collection including (*fo. 36*) a letter on the Guinea trade, n.d.   **2544**

Evreux

DEPARTMENTAL ARCHIVES

Archives départementales de l'Eure, 2 rue de la Préfecture, Evreux

The reading room is open from Monday to Saturday from 9 a.m. to 12 and from 2 to 6 p.m., except from July 1 to 15.

Etat sommaire des documents conservés aux archives du département de l'Eure, by M. Baudot, Evreux, 1939.

E 2759. Family papers (Delacroix) including some information about a **2545** slave ship, 1781–4.

E 3251. Family papers (François Saupin) including some information on the **2546** slave trade, 1711–71.

Grenoble

DEPARTMENTAL ARCHIVES

Archives départementales de l'Isère, Préfecture, place de Verdun, Grenoble

The reading room is open every day from 9 a.m. to 12 and from 2 to 5 p.m.

Catalogue général des manuscrits des bibliothèques publiques de France, vol. LI, Paris, 1956.

F 25. Part of a letter probably by Raby concerning a voyage to the West **2547** African coast, eighteenth century.

Honfleur

TOWN ARCHIVES

Archives municipales, Mairie, Honfleur, Calvados

It is advisable to write in advance for permission to see the documents. There are no fixed hours of opening.

Admiralty of Honfleur

Répertoire numérique des archives municipales de Honfleur, by A .Vintras, Caen, 1923.

There are 210 boxes of documents from 1636 to 1791, but the *Rapports de Mer*, in which most information about West Africa occurred, have been lost for the years after 1719. What survives consists of 22 registers of varying sizes (287–309) running from 1665 to 1719, but they contain no lists of subjects or indices, and there is no detailed inventory. They are extremely difficult to use.

E.g. *no. 290, fo. 6.* Report by Etienne Archer on his voyage to Senegal **2547a** from Le Havre with a cargo for the India Company, 13 November 1670.

fo. 6465. Report by Jacob Aldders of Dunkirk who had been to Guinea **2547b** for the India Company as a slaver, 26 June 1671.

ORDERS OF THE MARINE

464. Various papers, as of the slaver *Bonne Sophie*, 1784. **2548**

465. „ „ *Alexandrie, Prince Noir*, 1785. **2549**

466. „ „ *Deux soeurs unies, Prince Noir*, 1787. **2550**

467. „ „ *Asie, Elizabeth*, 1787. **2551**
E.g. Report on the slave ship, the *Asie*, about her trip to Guinea with a cargo to trade for 377 slaves, 1787. Report on the *Prince Noir* arriving from Guinea, 1787. Report on difficulties of the *Elizabeth* in the mouth of the river Calabar, 1787.

468. Various papers, as of the *Flore, Bonne Amitié*, 1788. **2552**

469. „ „ *Lion*, 1789. **2553**

XVI. VARIOUS SHIPS' PAPERS CLASSED BY NAME OF THE SHIP

630. Concerning the *Gracieuse* of Dieppe, catching turtles near Cape Verde, **2554** 1723–5.

645. Papers about the slave ship, the *Zéphir*, 1776–7. There may be further **2555** information in the notarial archives but they are entirely without indices or catalogues.[1]

[1] Maurice Delafosse, writing in vol. IV of the *Histoire des colonies françaises* under the editorship of Gabriel Hanotaux and Alfred Martineau, Paris, 1931, p. 7, mentions 30 vessels destined for West Africa in the notarial records between 1574 and 1583, but gives no exact reference.

Laon

Town Library

Bibliothèque de Laon, rue du Bornay, Laon, Aisne

The reading room is open every day from 9 a.m. to 12 and 1.30 to 6 p.m., and on Saturdays from 9 a.m. to 12.

Catalogue général des manuscrits des bibliothèques publiques de France, vol. XLI, Paris, 1903.

560. Register of correspondence relating to a regiment of Spahis in Senegal,   **2556**
   1842–8.

La Rochelle

i. Departmental Archives

Archives départementales de la Charente-Maritime, Place de la Préfecture, La Rochelle

The reading room is open from Monday to Friday from 9 a.m. to 12 and 2 to 6 p.m., and on Saturdays from 9 a.m. to 12.

There is a useful summary guide: M. Delafosse, *Guide des Archives de la Charente-maritime*, La Rochelle, 1958. Admiralty of *La Rochelle* Series B, 174–264, 5580–6094, and Marennes Series B 1–173, 6095–108. For the earlier numbers there is a printed inventory of the admiralty registers (B 1–283), M. Meschinet de Richemond, *Inventaire sommaire des Archives départementales antérieures à 1790, Charente Inférieure, Séries A–B*, La Rochelle, 1900. For the later numbers there are only a typewritten *répertoire numérique* of the briefest sort (B 5580–6127) and a manuscript *inventaire sommaire* for B 5580–B 5686 by F. de Vaux de Foletier and M. Delafosse. There is a manuscript index of the personal names of the Series B. A new *Répertoire numérique* for the whole of the Admiralty of La Rochelle is in preparation.

Series B. Amirauté de la Rochelle[1]

B. 26.   **2557**
E.g., *fo. 15 vo–16 vo*. Royal declaration on the price of Negroes to be paid
   by traders on the Guinea coast, 14 December 1716.

B. 32.   **2558**
E.g., *fo. 41 vo–44 vo*. Royal declaration concerning the Negro slaves in the
   colonies, 15 December 1738.

[1] See introduction to section on the archives of the Ministry of Marine, p. 89.

B. 46.   **2559**
E.g., *fo. 1 vo–3 vo.* Royal declaration on police control of Negroes, who are forbidden entrance to France, 9 August 1777.

B. 226.   **2560**
E.g., *fo. 1.* Permission given to a captain to land a Negro slave in France to have him instructed in the Catholic religion, 19 October 1737. Permits of this kind occur *passim.*

B. 234.   **2561**
E.g., *fo. 5–5 vo.* Appointment of Jean Joseph Lesenne to command the king's ship, *La Fille Unique,* on the African coast, 22 December 1785.

B. 247.   **2562**
E.g., *fo. 150 vo.* Declaration by Louis Daliveau, owner of the *Fortune,* travelling to Guinea, 17 March 1733. Such declarations occur *passim.*

B. 5592. Treatises and documents concerning Negroes and other coloured **2563** people, 1694, 1716, 1742, 1747, 1789.

B. 5913. Sale of the loot of the fort of Gambia in 1695–7. The fort had been **2564** taken by de Gennes on 17 July 1695. Inventory of the loot.
The registers with captains' reports (*rapports de mer*) have not been preserved.

Consular Jurisdiction of La Rochelle (B. 308–445, 4148–228)
There is a printed *Inventaire Sommaire* for *B. 308–445* and a manuscript *Répertoire numérique* for *B. 4148–228.* The documents are very difficult to use.

Family Papers (Series E, continued by the Series J.)

There is a printed *Inventaire Sommaire* for the earlier numbers and a *Réper-* **2565** *toire numérique* for the later ones. There is a general index of families on slips. *1.* L. De Richemond: *Inventaire sommaire des archives départementales antérieures à 1790, Charente Inférieure, Series C, D, E, G et H,* Paris, 1877 (Series E pp. 1–62). *2. Série E, Suite, no. E 250–535* (typewritten). *4. Répertoire numérique J* (typewritten). Includes, e.g., *E. 446–51.* Papers of the family Meschinet de Richemond, 1773–86. There was a well-known firm of slavers, de Richemond and Garnault.

II. TOWN ARCHIVES AND LIBRARY

Bibliothèque municipale, rue Gargoulleau, La Rochelle

The reading room is open every day from 2 to 6 p.m. The town librarian is also town archivist and the library and archives are closely connected; they are kept in the same building.

(1). Archives

L. Meschinet de Richemond: *Inventaire sommaire des archives départementales antérieures à 1790. Série E Supplément (Archives Communales), Ville de La Rochelle,* Paris, 1892 (there is no index).

E Supt 274 (old *E E 282* provisional pencil number *282*). Equipment and **2566** log-books of the *Roy Dahomet* navigating off the coast of Guinea under the command of Captain G. Corbie, 1772–4.

E Supt 274 (pencil number *283*). Log-books of the *Isle de France*, destined, **2567**
inter alia, for Goree on the African coast, 1790–1, contains an interesting
log-book by J. Crassous de Médeuil, the commanding officer, 1791.

(2). Library

G. Musset, *Catalogue général des manuscrits des bibliothèques publiques de France,
Départements*, vol. VIII, Paris, 1889. First supplement in: *Catalogue général des
manuscrits des bibliothèques publiques de France*, vol. XLI, *Supplément*, Paris, 1903.
Second supplement in: *Catalogue général des manuscrits des bibliothèques publiques de
France, Départements*, vol. XLVI, Paris, 1924, which goes as far as MS. 2137.
A manuscript supplement is being compiled by the librarian, Mlle. de Saint-
Affrique.

856. Log-book of the *Amitié*, belonging to Messrs. Rasseau brothers of La **2568**
Rochelle voyaging to Senegal, 5 November 1786 to 19 July 1792, includes
the story of a negro revolt, 4 May 1787.

1906. Collection of documents.   **2569**
     fo. 76–9. Navigation along the west coast of Africa by Albert Roussin,
captain of the *Bayadère* and the *Lévrier*, 1817 and 1818.
     fo. 81–104. Navigation on the coasts of West Africa from Cape
Bojador to Mount Souzos, hydrographic explorations carried out under
Roussin, 1817 and 1818.

1969 f. Accounts and other documents concerning the merchant fleet, n.d. **2570**

2271. Note on the articles which are suitable for trade on the coasts of **2571**
Africa from Cape Blanc to the river Saraillion, 5 folios, late eighteenth
century.

2289. Slaving voyages of the *Bonne Société*, for de Richemond and Gar- **2572**
nault of La Rochelle, 78 folios, 1781–9.
     2295 and *2296*, bound together:

2295, fo. 1–120. Documents concerning the *Baron de l'Espérance*, Captain **2573**
Banet, for de Richemond and Garnault, slavers at La Rochelle, trade
with Saint Pierre and Miquelon, 1784–7.

2296, fo. 1–272. Collection of documents concerning the slave trade from **2574**
the firm of de Richemond, Garnault and Company. Mainly accounts
and contracts, 1779–86.

2297. Documents from the firm of de Richemond, Garnault and Company, **2575**
equipment of (slave) ships, 1781–6.

III. CHAMBER OF COMMERCE
Chambre de Commerce, rue du Palais, La Rochelle

The reading room is open every day from 9 a.m. to 12 and from 2 to 6 p.m.,
and on Saturdays from 9 a.m. to 12. The very important archives of the *Chambre
de Commerce* of La Rochelle, founded in 1719, are divided in two parts, the
archives of the pre-revolutionary era and the more recent ones. The former are
again divided into original letters and documents received (of which there is an
excellent manuscript inventory), and the registers into which outgoing correspondence was copied (of which there is no inventory, but only alphabetical

tables in each volume). The whole of the archive is very well kept and classified.[1]
Permission to consult must be obtained from the President of the Chamber of
Commerce, rue du Palais, La Rochelle.

There is also a *Répertoire numérique*, typewritten, the documents being grouped
in boxes and dossiers with *Analyses détaillées*: five manuscript copybooks containing analyses of every document of the pre-1800 archives.

Box XIX: African trade and slave trade, documents 6511–767
The following are particularly interesting items in *Box XIX*, which is altogether
of the highest importance.

Dossier 1. Rules for the slave trade in Africa, place of trade, equipment of **2576**
the boats, 1736.

6511–29. Slave trade at Anamabou, royal protection for the trade in Guinea **2577**
and Goree. Abuses in Whydah, foreign competition, prices of slaves at **2578**
Cape Laho, goods suitable for the slave trade at Porto Novo and
Badagry, 1737.

6527. Letter from de la Luzerne, Minister of marine, stating that M. Gourg, **2579**
director of the factory at Whydah, has explained to him the advantages
of the slave trade at Porto Novo and Badagry on the Gold Coast over
Whydah where it is slackening, n.d.

Dossier 2:
E.g. Note on the equipment of slave ships at La Rochelle and in **2580**
other ports.
Statistical tables of the importation of Negroes in San Domingo.
Various statistics of the slave trade of great importance, *inter alia*, for
the Guinea coast, 1763 . . .

6503–45bis. Important statistical material. **2581**
E.g. *6545, 1789*, contains a calculation of the price of tonnage per head
of negro.

Dossier 3: 6546–9. Sea routes of the slavers on the African coast, 1786 . . . **2582**

Dossier 4: 6550. Salaries of the crews of the slave ships, 1787. **2583**

Dossier 5: 6551. E.g. Expedition of the Marquess de la Jaille to the coasts of **2584**
Africa to establish factories.
Documents concerning the archipelago of the Bissage, the Gold
Coast, Gambia (treaties with native kings), island of Idoles, Sierra
Leone and Benin, 1785.

Dossier 6: 6552–73. Privileges granted to certain commercial companies **2585**
and individuals for trading in Africa, *inter alia*, for trading in slaves,
and the construction of forts, 1721.

Dossier 7: 6574–643. Merchandise used in the slave trade. **2586**
Merchandise resulting from that trade and consumed in France, reduction of
import duties on it.

---

[1] E. Garnault, *Le commerce rochelais au XVIIIe siècle d'après les documents composant les
anciennes archives de la Chambre de Commerce de la Rochelle,* 5 vols., La Rochelle and Paris,
1888–1900.

Premiums and various advantages granted to the slavers, 1670 . . .

6586. E.g. Minutes of a meeting of traders held at Nantes about the contract by a slaver who had suffered heavy financial losses. 20 November 1739.

6619. Answer to three questions concerning the slave trade, asked by the Duc de Praslin. The answers deal mainly with English hostility and competition, the building of French forts on the Guinea coast and the necessity of official support for the trade; the role of brandy in dealing with the negroes is stressed, n.d.

6620. Another set of answers to the same questions, by E. Giraudeau, slaver, n.d.

6621. Another set of answers, by H. Massal, n.d.

6639. Extract of the statistics concerning negroes introduced into the colony of San Domingo in 1786 by French slavers; the *Comte de Forcalquier,* the *Reverseaux,* the *Argus,* the *Loudunois,* the *Cacique* and the *Aurore.* The coasts where the trade had taken place are indicated.

Dossier 8: 6644–58. Incidents between French and foreign boats on the African coasts, 1738. **2587**

Dossier 9: 6659–82. Complaints about captains and officers of slave ships by shipowners and others, 1773. **2588**

E.g. *6663.* Kidnapping of three free Christian Portuguese negroes of the island of Anamabou by Captain Blondeau of the *Comte de Jarnac,* s.d.

Dossier 10: 6666–82. Introduction of negroes into French and other colonies, 1673 . . . **2589**

Dossier 11: 6683–714. Papers concerning the slave trade at Ardres (Gold Coast) and Whydah. **2590**
French forts, protection of French ships.
Relations with the king of Ardres, invasion of his country by the king of Dahomey, 1787.
E.g. *6683.* Letter of M. de Warel, commanding fort St. Louis at Whydah, informing the Chamber of Commerce of talks with the new king of the Dahomets about trade between France and his country, 15 September 1774.
6909. Letter of M. Hardy, tradesman at Ardres about a certain Pierre, secretary of the king of Ardres educated in France, 5 September 1786.
6691. Copy of a letter from Pierre, secretary of the king of Ardres to the Marquess de Castries about a fort at Epée and at Porto Novo, 27 August 1786.
6694. Message from the king of Ardres and his ministers to the traders and shipowners of La Rochelle, 25 September 1787.
6697. Report from the officers of the *Solide* of La Rochelle, about Badagry and the king of Annis, 8 March 1788.
6713. Letter from the king of Ardres who promulgates certain measures which interest the traders of La Rochelle, 4 November 1790.

Dossier 12: 6715–67. Campaign of the Society of the Friends of the Negroes: abolition of the slave trade; troubles in the colonies, especially in San Domingo, 1789 . . . **2591**

DOCUMENTS: MANUSCRITS, APPENDICE

Box VI (Grand Bureau), 1

Two letters concerning the slave trade; one of them is addressed to the **2592**
merchants of La Rochelle and concerns the trade on the Guinea Coast
and the transport of slaves to San Domingo, n.d.

Box XIV. E. Documents concerning the tobacco trade.
    E.g. *4627, 4628.* Letters about the importance of tobacco in the **2593**
    slave trade, 27 September 1783.
    4808. Royal protection of trade and navigation in Guinea, 6 April
    1744).

Box XXI: Various documents on trade.
Dossier 8. General data on traffic in the port of La Rochelle. Statistics. **2594**
    E.g. *7317.* Concerns the African trade in 1753–4, 1764–5 and 1775–6.

Dossier 102. Letters concerning trade on the west coast of Africa, particu- **2595**
larly in Senegal, Gambia, Gulf of Guinea, Togo and the Cameroons.
Various dates.

Le Havre

1. TOWN ARCHIVES

Archives municipales, Hôtel de Ville, Le Havre

The reading room is open to the public from Monday to Friday from 8.30 a.m.
to 12, and from 2 to 6 p.m., and on Saturday from 8.30 a.m. to 12. For the pre-
revolutionary period there is an inventory: *Archives municipales antérieures à 1790*,
by Ph. Barrey and L. Préteux, Le Havre, 1930. For the revolutionary period:
Archives municipales de la période révolutionnaire, by Ph. Barrey and L. Préteux,
Le Havre, 1930.

PRE-REVOLUTIONARY PERIOD

HH 67. Colonial Trade. **2596**
Inter alia. Papers concerning the commercial conference of Versailles about
    the use of indigo in West Africa, 1775.
Request for the suppression of monopoly trading in Senegal, 1773–90.

HH 69, 70. Colonial Trade. **2597**
Inter alia. Register of names of French ships going to the West African
    coast and the nature of their cargo, 1763–93.

HH 72. Slave Trade. **2598**
Inter alia. Papers about the supply of slaves by foreigners, 1762.
The numbers of slaves carried by ships from Le Havre, 1762.

Request by a merchant from Honfleur for permission to ship cider to Guinea, 1764.

Dues on slaves, 1767.

Copy of a letter about the frauds practised by a slave captain, 1771.

Request for free trade in Senegal, 1741–86.

HH 73. Slave Trade.   **2599**

The accounts of the captain of a slaver, 1774–92.

REVOLUTIONARY PERIOD

F^2 7. Papers about trade with *inter alia*, West Africa, 1783.   **2600**

F^2 9. Papers concerning colonial trade, 1789–*An* III.   **2601**

F^2 89. Register containing notes on the provisions necessary for the voy- **2602**
age to Senegal, n.d.

II. Town Library
Bibliothèque municipale du Havre, 2bis rue Ancelot, Le Havre

The reading room is open every day from 9 a.m. to 12 and from 2 to 6 p.m.

Catalogue général des manuscrits des bibliothèques publiques de France, vol. II, 299–346, Le Havre (1000), Paris, 1888. *Supplément*, vol. XLI, 531–43, Paris, 1903.

210. (A2) Eyriès Collection. *Inter alia, fo. 153.* Two letters about the **2603**
Compagnie de Sénégal, by Jacques Paulze, 1775–7.

245. (A9) Collection of Spanish maps (*inter alia, 6.* Senegal and Guinea, **2604**
n.d. *7.*-Congo and Gabon, n.d.).

516. Log-book of the *Rosalie* of Le Havre for Angola by David Osmond, **2605**
eighteenth century.

517. Log-book of the *Roy d'Angolle* for Angola by Osmond, 1792.   **2606**

537. Accounts of Chevalier Boufflers, from Senegal, 1787.   **2607**

444. Manuscripts of J. B. Eyriès, 1767–1864 (*inter alia, 18.* Papers about **2608**
Africa, n.d.).

445. 11bis. Progress of geographical knowledge of Africa until the first **2609**
Portuguese discoveries, n.d.

12. Travels by Pruneau de Pommegorge, Adanson and Demanet in Africa, **2610**
n.d.

13. Travels on the West African coast between Cape Blanc and the **2611**
Guinea Coast, n.d.

14. Translation from English into French of a report on Sierra Leone, 1827. **2612**

15. Note on the natives of Sierra Leone, n.d.   **2613**

Le Mans

DEPARTMENTAL ARCHIVES

Archives départementales de la Sarthe, rue des Résistants-Internés, Le Mans

The reading room is open every day from Monday to Friday from 9 a.m. to 12 and from 2 to 6 p.m., and on Saturday from 9 a.m. to 12 and from 2 to 4 p.m.

4E. Fonds Bourges de la Flèche, documents of de la Rivière, 1787–92. **2614**

Lorient

ARCHIVES OF THE PORT OF LORIENT

Archives du Port Militaire de Lorient, Bibliothèque du Port, Lorient

Application must be made to the *Service Historique de la Marine, 3 avenue Octave Gréard, Paris VIIe* for permission to consult these archives. They are kept in the Library of the Port and may be seen any day between 8.30 and 11.45 a.m. and 1.15 and 7 p.m., except on Saturdays when the library shuts at 5.30 p.m. It is wise to make a written appointment.

One series of documents of interest for West Africa is kept here: the archives of the India Company during the eighteenth century: see A. Legrand: *Inventaire des archives de la Compagnie des Indes, Extrait du Bulletin de la Section de Géographie.* Paris, 1913.[1] A supplement appeared in 1932: *Supplément à l'inventaire du fonds de la Compagnie des Indes*, by F. Marec, Paris, 1932.

Carton 270–8. Papers of the Senegalese ports of the Company. **2615**
    E.g., carton 274 (Marec: 92), dossier 1. Details of dues paid to the natives in Senegal, 1722–52.
    carton 278, dossier 1. Letters from St. Robert, the company's agent in Senegal about slavery, the gum trade etc., 1725.
    (Marec 96). Tables of the professions, salaries etc. of the employees of the company in Whydah, Guinea and Senegal, eighteenth century.

---

[1] There were three India Companies: of the first there are no archives; those of the second are in Lorient; of the third, in the *Archives Nationales*.

Lyons

ARCHIVES AND LIBRARY OF THE MISSION FOR
THE PROPAGATION OF THE FAITH

Oeuvres pontificales missionnaires de la Propagation de la Foi et de Saint Pierre-Apôtre
Bibliothèque et archives, 31 rue du Plat, Lyons

The archives may be consulted from Monday to Friday from 8 to 11.45 a.m. and from 2 to 5.45 p.m. They belong to the organization supporting all French catholic missionary activity founded in 1822 and which has a further centre in Paris: *rue Monsieur, Paris VIIe*.

Together these two centres issue two periodicals: *Annales de la Propagation de la Foi*, Lyons, 1853 *et seq.*, some of which contain tables of contents and of which volumes of indices have appeared: *Tables des Annales de la Propagation de la Foi, 1822–53*, Lyons, 1853; *1853–74*, Lyons, 1874; *1874–1903*, Lyons, Paris, 1904. Translations of many of these volumes have appeared in German, Italian, English, Dutch etc. They print the texts of many documents from the archives either in Lyons or Paris from 1822 onwards, although they are not exhaustive. A further publication by the society is: *Les Missions Catholiques*, Lyons, Paris, 1868 *et seq.*, which prints similar material, and which contains tables of contents. There is no inventory or repertory of these archives.

The territories in West Africa in which the Society is interested include: Guinea (Fathers of the Holy Spirit, mission begun 1840); Dahomey (Missions Africaines de Lyon, 1860); Senegambia (Fathers of the Holy Spirit, 1861); Senegal (Fathers of the Holy Spirit, 1866). There are three groups of archive material.

I. *Series of boxes*, numbered chronologically containing groups of docu-   **2616**
ments grouped geographically. They contain letters and reports sent to
the Society from missionaries in all parts of the world. Some have been
printed in the *Annales*.

II. *Registers of minutes* of the meetings of the directors of the Society in   **2617**
Lyons from 1822 onwards. These have no indices but occasional rubrics
serve as a partial guide to their contents.

III. *Registers of letters* despatched from the directors in Lyons, *inter alia*, to the   **2618**
various missions. There are partial lists of these letters.

IV. *Financial reports*, issued from time to time, e.g., in 1855, 1875, etc.   **2619**

V. *Varia* including a printed volume of analyses of information sent back   **2620**
by the various missions:
    E.g., containing figures of population; Catholic, heretic, infidel; con-
versions; clergy: European and indigenous; churches and chapels;
schools; hospitals etc.

Marseilles

I. DEPARTMENTAL ARCHIVES
Archives départementales des Bouches du Rhône, Préfecture, Marseille

The reading room is open from Monday to Friday between 8.30 a.m. and 12, and from 2.30 to 6 p.m. and on Saturdays from 8.30 a.m. to 12.

There is a useful guide to these archives by R. Busquet, *Les fonds des archives départementales des Bouches du Rhône*, first volume, *Dépôt principal de Marseille. Séries anciennes A à F*. Marseille, 1937. Two further fascicules 1939 and 1954. Material concerning West Africa is most likely to be found in the archives of the *Amirauté: Inventaire sommaire des archives départementales antérieures à 1790: Bouches du Rhône. Archives civiles—Série B, Tome IV, Amirauté de Marseille et des mers du Levant* by R. Busquet, Marseille, 1932. This consists of an *Etat sommaire* of the archives of the various *amirautés* and of a detailed inventory of the first six numbers 1XB1–1XB6 concerning Marseilles and of number 1XB 171. From the other material it is extremely difficult to extract relevant information.

Series IXB. *Amirauté de Marseille*

2. *fo. 680.* Royal permission for a ship to be loaded with iron in Catalonia **2621** for the West African coast, 1647.

4. *fo. 126 vo.* Permission for the *Hirondelle*, Captain Cazalis to trade in **2622** Guinea in slaves, gold dust etc., 1702.

5. *fo. 777.* Same, for the *Mars*, Captain Cazejus, 1727. **2623**
   fo. 864. Same, for the *Junon*, owner G. Gameau, 1729.
   fo. 1296. Same, for the *Marie-Thérèse*, Captain Manen, s.d.

6. *fo. 8v.* Same, for the *Saint-Philippe*, Captain J. Pelisner, 1730. **2624**
   fo. 163. Same, for Captain Bremond, 1734.
   fo. 240. Same, for the *Dauphin*, Captain J.-A. Richard, 1735.
   fo. 253v. Same, 1735.
   fo. 264. Same, for owners Rocante and Figuières, 1736.
   fo. 262. Edict about the stay of slaves in France and their transport to the colonies, 1716.
   fo. 839. Permission to L.-A. Isnardon to bring a native boy, Titus, from Congo to learn to be a cook, 1744. (This is one of several similar grants.)

Series XXXIX E.

103. This collection of commercial documents contains one register of the **2625** archives of the Régis Company which was interested in trade on the African coast, 1847–8. (The rest of the archive has disappeared.)

II. CHAMBER OF COMMERCE OF MARSEILLE
Chambre de commerce de Marseille, Palais de la Bourse

It is necessary to write to the archivist for permission to see the documents.

There is a *Répertoire numérique des archives de la Chambre de commerce de Marseille, Tome Ier, archives antérieures à 1801, Fonds particulier de la Chambre* by J. Reynaud, Marseille, 1947, which notes the volumes destroyed in 1944. The very rich nineteenth-century archives have not as yet been inventoried.

Series AA.

107. Report on de la Jaille's mission on the *Emeraude* and the *Levrette* to find   **2626**
suitable trading posts on Bissage, the Gold Coast, Gambia, Sierra Leone, 1785.

109. Information about the slave trade on the African coast especially   **2627**
round Cape Laho, 1787.

Series H.

2. Reports by Captain Broquant and Bouët-Willaumez on the slave trade   **2628**
and coasts between Gallinas and Gabon, 1839.

Nantes

1. DEPARTMENTAL ARCHIVES

Archives départementales, communales et hospitalières de la Loire-Atlantique, 8 rue de Bouillé, Nantes

These archives are open from Monday to Friday, from 9.30 a.m. until 12, and from 2 until 6 p.m. and on Saturdays from 9.30 a.m. to 12, except from July 1 to 15. There is a most useful *Guide des Archives de la Loire-Atlantique*, by H. de Berranger, vol. I Series A to H, Nantes, 1962, and a second volume concerning the Series I to Z and the Fonds Marine is in preparation. There is a repertory of the admiralty archives: *Archives départementales de la Loire-Inférieure (antérieures à 1790): Repertoire numérique de la Série B (Cours et Juridictions)*, Nantes, 1945. This contains only the briefest information and no more extensive analysis of the documents has been undertaken in full although some have been used by Gaston Martin: *L'ère des négriers (1714–74)*, Paris, 1931 (vol. 2 of *Nantes au XVIIIe siècle*).

Admiralty Archives (*Amirauté de Nantes*)[1]

B 4512–B 4614. Register of statements by ship-owners, captains, ships'   **2629**
surgeons, negroes etc., 1740–93.

---

[1] These archives have been extensively used by L. Vignols. See section on the Departmental Archives in Rennes, and p. 89.

E.g. *B. 4515*. Lists some of its contents inside the front and back covers but this is very incomplete and such volumes may easily contain other information about West Africa and particularly about the slave trade, e.g., fo. 179 the arrival of a slave in France.

B 4570–96. Registers of the reports of captains returning from voyages, **2630** 1699–1779. This is by far the most interesting group of documents for the history of West Africa in this archive, but unfortunately there is no analysis of it. Many of the entries concern the slave trade and each item is noted in the margins according to the name of the ship concerned.

E.g. *B 4581 fo. 27*. Report that the *Hardi* has been captured by pirates off the West African coast and held for a ransom of £800 gold dust, 27 January 1723.

B 4582. fo. 138, 139. Report on troubles of the *Légère* of Nantes with its crew and agents in Rufisque, 25 October 1726.

B 4584. fo. 60v. Report on the pillaging of the cargo of the *Charlemagne* by natives of Dahomey, 7 July 1729.

B 4588. fo. 49. Report of Captain Ollier of the *Mentor* of the presence of a native hostage taken in Loango because natives had stolen some slaves and goods, 21 June 1740.

B 4592. fo. 63. Description of the slaving voyage of the *Sirène*, 13 May 1754.

B 4594. fo. 64. Report of attack on the *Marie* off Goree, 3 June 1768.

fo. 114. Report on the capture of the crew of the *Furet* in the river Bursalamur. The ship's stores had been stolen and it filled with water, 21 April 1769.

B 4595. fo. 8. Report of the revolt of forty-eight slaves of the *Entreprise* off the Gold Coast and the assassination of almost all the crew by two other slaves sold to the captain by King Dimby, 18 April 1771.

B 4596. fo. 4. Report of attack on the *Jean-Baptiste* in the river Gambia, trading in wax, ivory and slaves, by natives and others who claimed to be Portuguese and who later captured the ship, its captain and some of the crew, 1 June 1775.

fo. 113. Description of the mutiny of the second officer of the *Aimable française*, Captain Perroty, in Portugal, 23 August 1777.

B 5004–6. Log-books (Journaux de bord).

B 5004. Log-book of Le Breton Lavallée which includes sketches of the **2631** West African coast, 1753.[1]

B 5006. Two log-books kept by Dam Joulin on voyages to Guinea, the **2632** Gold Coast and Whydah, 1743–5; 1745 (in great detail).[2]

Marine Archives (*Fonds Marine*)

This collection includes
(1) the records of the registration of merchant shipping (*Inscription Maritime*) of Nantes abolished in 1934.
(2) same, for the Quartier of Nantes.
(3) same, for Le Croisic.
(4) same, for Saint-Nazaire.

[1] Edited by J. Mousnier: *Journal de la Traite des Noirs*, Paris, 1957.
[2] *Ibid.*

Nineteenth-century inventories of this collection have become useless because of the many losses, but there is a card index by name of ship and date: *Répertoire sur fiches* by H. de Berranger, 1951–2, and for naval ships the *Répertoire des journaliers d'armement des bâtiments d'Etat* (1745–1861), by G. Beauchesne. The collection records the crew, cargo, and equipment of ships, and includes some leaving for West Africa. At present, however, it is difficult to trace such information unless the date and the name of the ship are known.

Section 1. (above) includes about 300 lists of crews of naval ships, 1745– **2633** 1861.

Section 2. Crew, cargo and equipment records, 1779–1812.   **2634**

Section 3. Crew, cargo and equipment records, 1700–87.   **2635**

Series J. Collection of Family Papers[1]

8. J. Delaville-Deguer collection 1758–1839   **2636**
This collection of the papers of the ship-owner Prudent Delaville and his brother-in-law François Deguer, and from 1763 onwards of the latter alone, may contain information about West Africa, as the firm participated in trade there, but there is no inventory of its contents.

1–9. Copies of outgoing correspondence, 1763–82.[2]   **2637**
    E.g., *vol. 5: fo. 102*. Letter recording the arrival of 487 out of cargo of 526 slaves, 22 April 1769.

10–11. Ships fitted out etc., 1764–80.   **2638**

12–22. Account books (receipts), 1801–39, 1761–87.   **2639**

23–5. Record of daily payments, 1768–70, 1773–9.   **2640**

26–9. Various.   **2641**

16. J. Berthrand de Coeuvres Collection

1. Dossiers about ships, 1757–92.   **2642**

2–3. Maritime insurance and accounts, 1757– *An* V.   **2643**

4. Correspondence received, 1763–95.   **2644**

5–7. Accounts, 1737–96.   **2645**

8. Fragment of register of outgoing correspondence, 1765–83.   **2646**

9. Log-book of the slaver the *Reine des Anges*, Captain Philippe Hanion de **2647** Courchamp, on voyage to Anamabou, describing the negotiations and amounts paid in dues at the different ports for the purchase of 407 slaves, 1741–2.

1. JJ. Chaurand frères collection[3]

1–8. Copies of letters to America, unbroken series, 1782–93.   **2648**
9–25. Copies of letters to Europe, 1779–93.   **2649**

---

[1] *Répertoire dactylographié de la Série J*, by S. Canal and H. de Berranger (continuous from 1938 onwards). These manuscripts have been extensively used by D. Rinchon: *Les armements négriers au XVIIIe siècle*, in *Académie royale des sciences coloniales, classe des sciences morales et politiques, Nouvelle série, T. VII, fasc. 3*, Brussels, 1956.

[2] These volumes contain tables of the correspondents involved.

[3] This collection has been extensively used by D. Rinchon, *op. cit.*

26–8. Record of commissioning and laying up of ships, 1774–92. **2650**
    It is in these volumes that details of cargoes, crews and ships may be discovered.
29. Lost.

30–81. Various: chiefly accounts. **2651**

Chamber of Commerce (*Chambre de Commerce*)

Inventaire sommaire des archives départementales antérieures à 1790: Loire-Inférieure: Tome II.—deuxième partie: Séries C et D, by L. Maitre, Nantes, 1898.

C *587.* Register, 1764–7. **2652**
    E.g. List of ships sent to the Guinea coast. Copy of dues possibly required to be paid for participation in the slave trade.

C. *589.* Register, 1774–8. **2653**
    E.g. Memorandum protesting about the capture of a vessel by the Portuguese off the Guinea Coast.

C. *596.* Register, 1730–3. **2654**
    E.g. Copies of letters about the trade in brandy with America and Guinea.

C. *598.* Register, 1737–44. **2655**
    E.g. Copies of letters about the precautions necessary against the English in West Africa.

C. *599.* Register, 1744–9. **2656**
    E.g. Copies of letters about complaints of privilege in the African trade.

C *602.* Register, 1762–7. **2657**
    E.g. Copies of letters about ships sent from Nantes to Guinea and the numbers of slaves who could be introduced into the colonies. Draft of regulations for the colonial trade.

C *604.* Register, 1771–6. **2658**
    E.g., *fo. 156.* Copies of letters about the favour shown to the English by the King of Dahomey who had complained about the quality of the rifles sent him but who seems in fact to have been using them badly, 1775. (Contains alphabetical table of contents.)

C *607.* Register, 1783–8. **2659**
    E.g. Copies of letters about the concession of the gum monopoly of Senegal to the Company of Guyane.

C *615.* Packet, 1738–44. **2660**
    E.g. Correspondence received, *inter alia,* about English opposition to French trade in Guinea, and the manufacture of rifles for Guinea.

C *616.* Packet, 1745–50. **2661**
Correspondence received, *inter alia,* about tobacco for Guinea.

C *621.* Packet, 1773–5. **2662**
Correspondence received, *inter alia,* about the consequences of rivalry between French captains on the Guinea Coast.

C 687 (Carton 22, cotes 3–7).   **2663**
    E.g. Letters to the Admiralty office of Nantes about hostilities of the
English on the Guinea Coast, 1737–59.

C 699 (Carton 27, cotes 1).   **2664**
    E.g. Memorandum on the measures to be taken to encourage the
Guinea trade, 1748.

C 727 (Carton 34, cotes 1–4), 1696–1788.   **2665**
    E.g. Memorandum from St. Louis about the slave trade and the
barter goods desired by the King of Dahomey, 1773.

C 738 (Carton 38, cote 1). Companies, 1761–1790.   **2666**
    E.g. Regulation of trade until 1690. Regulations for the Guinea Com-
pany which is to trade in slaves, gold etc.(1685). Conditions for the
supply of 4,000 slaves for Compagnie d'Asient, 1701. The transference
of such privileges to the Compagnie des Indes (1720). Sketch map of
Africa, 1716. Concession of all trade in the slaves, arms etc. in Africa to
the later (1722). Account of slaving voyage, 1732. Report of 110 slaves
dead on voyage, 1739. Concession of £13 per head for each slave transported to the Islands, 1744. Memoranda etc. sent to Choiseul by merchants from Nantes about trade to Africa in the country's resources,
1762. Memorandum on trade in Calabar, 1762. Report by Captain
Blondeau on a voyage to the African coast, 1775. Protests about acts of
violence by the Portuguese in West Africa (n.d.). Navigational information (n.d.). List of Companies' ships engaged in the triangular voyage,
1767. Memorandum by the merchants of Nantes with a view to establishing trading posts in West Africa, 1777. Complaints by various
merchants against the Portuguese invasion of Cabinda, 1783. Treaty
with the King of Anamabou for the establishment of a French fort, 1786.
Statement by the ministers of the King of Ardres explaining the actions
of King Dahomet's men, 1788. Note on the importance of the colonies
and the slave trade, 1789, etc.

C 739 (Carton 38, cotes 2–3).   **2667**
Trade with the African coast, 1684–1787.
    E.g. Papers about the rights of the Compagnie de Sénégal, 1684.
Regulations about trade in Senegal, the African coast and the American
Islands, n.d. The establishment of a new royal company of Senegal,
Cape Verde and the African coast, 1696. Payments for taking part in the
slave or gold trades, n.d. Monopoly of slave trade in Goree and on the
African coast for the Compagnie de Guyane, 1777. Its replacement by a
monopoly of the gum trade in the Senegal river, 1784. Papers about the
despatch of brandy to Africa, 1689 and 1701. Memorandum by André
Brüe on ways of increasing trade with Africa, and a list of prices for
goods there, 1702. Report on Whydah and the Guinea trade, 1732.
Papers about the possibility of constructing a fort in the river Formosa,
n.d. Report on the monopoly of slave trade in the kingdoms of Benin and
Ouerre, n.d. Numerous geographical details about the valleys of Benin
and Wari, n.d. Papers about the Asiento treaty, 1701, etc.

C 740 (Carton 38, cotes 4–5). The Guinea Trade, 1713–89.   **2668**
    E.g. Papers about free trade in Guinea, 1716. Papers about obtaining

slaves, s.d. Various papers about participation in the slave trade, 1719, 1722, 1741, 1748, 1767. Permit granted to the *Duc de Bretagne*, 1713. Memorandum about restricting the number of those trading in Guinea, 1713. Papers advising against trade monopolies in Guinea, s.d. Justification of the behaviour of captains on the coast of Senegal, s.d. List of boats sent from Nantes to Guinea, 1748–75. Memorandum on the slave trade, s.d. Papers about European goods for the African trade, 1755, 1767, 1769. List of goods necessary to carry on the slave trade for one year and more suitable for barter, 1704, etc.

C 741 (Carton 38, cote 6). The Slave Trade, 1688–1789.   **2669**
Documents consisting for the most part of details about the different amounts of dues payable by those participating in the slave trade.

C 742 (Carton 38, cotes 7–8). The Slave Trade, 1716–90.   **2670**
    E.g. Various papers about the rights of slaves brought to France, 1716, 1783. Papers from the Admiralty office of Nantes forbidding them to be sent back to the colonies, 1770. Various papers about foreign participation in the slave trade to the French colonies, 1761, 1783, etc.

II. Town Archives
Archives municipales, rue Garde Dieu, Nantes

The municipal archives are open to the public between 9 a.m. and 12, except between July 12 and August 12.

There is a printed inventory by S. de la Nicollière-Teijeiro: *Inventaire-sommaire des archives communales antérieures à 1790. Ville de Nantes.* Three vols. Nantes, 1888–1919. *Table générale* by René Blanchard, brought up to date by M. Giraud-Mangin, Nantes, 1948.

D. 950. Dossier containing list of seeds and exotic plants which were to be   **2671**
asked from ships' captains going to West Africa for the apothecaries' garden, 1726–8.

FF. 199. Dossier containing list of seeds and vegetables exported from   **2672**
Nantes, *inter alia*, for Guinea, 1720.

FF. 202. Complaints from the merchants of Nantes against the monopoly   **2673**
of the Compagnie des Indes of the African trade, n.d.

HH. 221. Dossier containing, *inter alia*, decision to send fewer cowries to   **2674**
Guinea as they had become less popular there, 1721.

HH. 236. Dossier containing, *inter alia*, ordinance forbidding slaves to mass   **2675**
on the quays in Nantes, 1762.
    Difficulties with the Compagnie des Indes, 1720. Freedom to trade there, 1725. Report on the defeat of the King of Whydah by Dada Fidalgue, King of Dahomey, 1727. Various royal edicts about the slave trade, n.d.

HH. 268. Seizure of native-made carpets from Guinea by customs, 1722–3.   **2676**

H. 148. Insurance for Berthrand de Coeuvres in the *Prince Noir* on a slaving   **2677**
voyage to Guinea and St. Domingue, n.d.

III. Town Library

Bibliothèque publique, rue Gambetta, Nantes

The library is open every day from 9.30 to 12 and from 2 to 6 p.m. Its manuscript collection is listed in *Catalogue général des bibliothèques publiques de France, Départements, 8° Séries*, Vol. XXII. Paris, 1893. Further references must be added from the catalogue in the library in order to obtain the documents.

C. *11. 878. fo. 1–13v.* Remarks on the Gold Coast from Arguin to Patugris, **2678**
including short descriptions of Senegal, Cape Verde, Goree, River
Gallinas, Grand Bassam, River de Sestos, Baffa, Cape Palmas, Fort
Chana, Queta, Grand Popo, Whydah, eighteenth century.

fo. 14. Remarks on the dues to be paid at Whydah: e.g., what must be **2679**
be given to Dada, King of Dahomey in Anamabou, and to King Champeau in Petit Popo.

fo. 18. Accounts of a slaving voyage to Whydah in 1767 and Porto **2680**
Novo, 1770.

fo. 25. Note on how to care for slaves on the sea crossing, n.d.   **2681**

C. *19. 1803.* Note by de la Jaille on Senegal, with a fairly detailed descrip- **2682**
tion of the commercial possibilities there, 1784. Manuscript map of the
islands des Idoles, off the West African coast, 1785.

Poitiers

I. Departmental Archives

Archives départementales de la Vienne, rue Edouard-Grimaux, Poitiers

The reading room is open from Monday to Friday from 8.30 a.m. to 12 and
2 to 6.30 p.m. and contains the archives of the *Société des Antiquaires de l'Ouest*
in which the following manuscript is to be found:

116, 138. Mélanges Bonsergent, including the description of a voyage to Senegal
by Rubaud, 1786.

II. Town Library

Bibliothèque municipale, place Notre-Dame, Poitiers

The reading room is open every day between 9.30 and 11.30 a.m., and 2 and
6 p.m., except Sunday, Monday and July 1–15.
    Catalogue général des manuscrits des bibliothèques publiques de France, vol. XXV,
Paris, 1894.

287. Description of French trade in Senegal, Guinea and the Gold Coast, **2683** eighteenth century.

289 (21). Description of European trade in Asia, Africa and America, 1706. **2684**

Quimper

DEPARTMENTAL ARCHIVES

Archives départementales de Finistère, 4 rue du Palais, Quimper

The archives are open to the public from 9 a.m. to 12, and from 2 to 6 p.m. from Monday to Friday, and from 9 a.m. to 12 on Saturday, except July 1–15.

There is an *Inventaire sommaire des archives départementales antérieures à 1790. Finistère. Archives civiles; Série B. Tome III articles B 4160–4670, Inventaire des fonds des Amirautés de Morlaix, Quimper, du Consulat et du Tribunal de commerce de Morlaix*, by J. Lemoine and H. Bourde de la Rogerie, Quimper, 1902.

Series B. (*Amirauté*)

B. 4177. Register of minutes of the admiralty of Morlaix refers to the sale **2685** of a slave ship, the *Triomphant*, 1754.

B. 4187. Monopoly of the slave trade in the kingdoms of Ouaire and **2686** Benin, granted to Brillantois Marion and Co., of St. Malo, 1786.

Rennes

DEPARTMENTAL ARCHIVES

Archives départementales d'Ille-et-Vilaine, 2 place Saint-Mélaine, Rennes

The reading room is open to the public every day between 9 a.m. and 12, and from 2.30 to 5.30 p.m., except from July 1 to July 15.

Series 1 B. *Edits, déclarations, arrêts du Conseil*

There are two eighteenth-century manuscript guides without indexes to this series but however, there is a modern card index of subjects. It is, still, however, very difficult to extract information from this source.

[1] See introductory note to the section on the Archives of the Ministry of Marine, p. 89.

33/184 vo. Edict about slaves in the colonies, October 1716.   **2687**

33/190 vo. Declaration about the value of male and female child slaves,   **2688**
14 December 1716.

38/45 vo. Royal declaration about the treatment of slaves, 15 December   **2689**
1738.

44/22 vo. Royal proclamation for the control of natives, 9 August 1777.   **2690**

Same. Edict concerning the return of negroes to the colonies, 7 September   **2691**
1771.

Series 9 B. *Amirauté de St. Malo*

All the archives of the Admiralty of St. Malo are now in the departmental
archives in Rennes. There is a guide by H.-F. Buffet: *Archives départementales d'Ille-
et-Vilaine. Répertoire numérique de la sous-série 9 B: amirauté de Saint-Malo*, Rennes,
1962.

For the first ninety-seven numbers there is an inventory: *Inventaire sommaire
des archives départementales antérieures à 1790:*

Série B. Numbers 1 to 9 concern ordinances etc. and numbers 9–122,   **2692**
judicial processes.

    E.g. *1. fo. 51vo.* Report on the seizure of a Dutch ship on the way to
Guinea, 1694.

    2. fo. 15. Report on passports for the Guinea trade, 1715. It is very difficult
to extract information from the volumes 9 to 122.[1]

For information about West Africa the most promising source is 9 B. 436–   **2693**
555: registers of captains of ships from St. Malo, St. Briac, Cancale,
Vivier, 1678–1788.

    E.g. *9 B 505.* Description of the *Ruby*'s part in the slave trade in Angola,
by her captain, 1752.

Series C.

For the series of the *Intendance* and *Etats* of Brittany there is a printed inventory:
*Inventaire sommaire des archives départementales antérieures à 1790, Archives civiles,
Série C*, by M. E. Quesnet, P. Parfouru, A. Lesort and H. Bourde de la Rogerie.
Three volumes. Rennes, 1878–1934. These volumes contain no indexes but there
is a card index of subjects in the reading room.

C 29. Dossier containing, *inter alia*, letters about the supply of rifles from   **2694**
Nantes for Guinea, 1736.

C 1584. Various letters concerning the slave trade, 1762.   **2695**

C 3839. Register containing, *inter alia*, p. 93: complaints about the condi-   **2696**
tion of the slave trade by Nantes, 1787.

C 3893. Two dossiers about the slave trade, *inter alia*, about the payment   **2697**
of dues, 1786–9.

C 3928. Dossier containing, *inter alia*, a printed request for a ship to open up   **2698**
more of the coast of Angola for the slave trade, 1776.

---

[1] They were however used by L. Vignols: 'La campagne négrière de *La Perle*, 1755–
1757', in the *Revue Historique*, vol. clxiii, 1930, employing, however, a provisional
classification of documents.

Series 1 F XXI. *Fonds Vignols*

1930. Articles and notes by Léon Vignols, including résumés of articles and **2699**
books, *inter alia*: Crew rosters for Guinea.
List of boats fitted out in St. Malo, 1706–39.
Report of Captain Jean Poitevin, pirate, 1695.

1932. Text, annotations, etc. of book '*La Traite des nègres au XVIIIe s.*, **2700**
surtout par Nantes et Saint-Malo de 1725 à 1741'.

1933. Notes from archives and libraries, on the slave trade. **2701**

1940. Same, for Senegal and neighbouring countries. **2702**
This contains notes from: *Arch. municipales de Bordeaux.*
Two pieces concerning ship for gum trade in Senegal, 1800.
Copy of document from Series C (non-classée) on Senegal.
Copy of description of St. Louis, 1842, from Vignol's own collection.

Series 4 Fg : *Marine and Colonies*

There is a typed guide to this series, with a supplement.

144. Papers of Antonio-José dà Cumba. **2703**
This small collection of documents concerns the captain, Antonio-José dà
Cumba, of a Spanish slave ship, the *Notre-Dame de la Conception*, and
includes some cargo lists including slaves bought in Loango, 1783–6.

12. Cargo of goods for slave trade of Jean Lacotte, who embarked on the **2704**
Diligent of St. Malo, for a voyage to Guinea and Martinique, 1740.

42. Papers of Jean and René Ballan, merchants and ship-owners of Nantes, **2705**
concerning, *inter alia*, the *Victoire* (Captain La Barre-Proust) 1764, for
slave trade.

The *Saint-Domingue* (Jean Bordage) slaver 1774–6, captured by Portuguese **2706**
at Casamance.

The *Deux-Amis* (Captain Mathurin Banand) slaver, 1778–80. **2707**

Bailli de Suffren (Captain Joseph Gallan) slaver, n.d. **2708**
Bonne-Mère, 1787.

Papers of slaver, with names of native middle-men, numbers of slaves etc., **2709**
1768.

45. Papers of Apuril de Kerloguen of St. Malo, about the *Henry IV* **2710**
(Captain de Kerusec), the *Magdeleine* (Captain Darthiague), the *Madame*,
fitted out by Delaville of Nantes, slave traders, 1783.

87. Various papers about the slave trade. **2711**

Rochefort

ARCHIVES OF THE PORT OF ROCHEFORT

Archives du Port militaire de Rochefort, Charente-Maritime

The consultation of this archive is extremely difficult. It consists of a small series of seventeenth-century registers of which there is a *Répertoire numérique des archives de l'arrondissement maritime de Rochefort*, by D. Lemoine, Paris, 1925.

Series R. *Colonies, foreign countries, consulates*

59. Documents concerning Guinea, 1701.			**2712**
60. „ „ Senegal, An VIII.			**2713**

Rouen

I. DEPARTMENTAL ARCHIVES

Archives départementales de la Seine-Maritime, 21 rue de Crosne, Rouen

The reading room is open to the public from Monday to Friday from 9 a.m. to 12 and from 2 to 6 p.m., and on Saturday from 9 a.m. to 12, from July 1 to 15.

In principle the Admiralty documents (Amirauté de Rouen, de Deippe, du Havre) are preserved here, but they await new premises and are almost impossible to consult. All these series, which are considerable, have not been inventoried, except for a list of the documents of the Admiralty of Dieppe, by M. Darsel.[1] The documents of the Consulate of Rouen (the beginnings of the Chamber of Commerce) are also very extensive, but still without inventory. The archives of the Chamber of Commerce were for the most part destroyed during the war.[2]

II. TOWN LIBRARY

Bibliothèque municipale, 3 rue de la Bibliothèque, Rouen

The reading room is open from Monday to Saturday from 10 a.m. to 12, and from 2 to 7 p.m. except from July 15 to August 15.

Catalogue général des manuscrits des bibliothèques publiques de France, vol. I, Rouen, 1886, with supplements in vol. XLIII (1904), and vol. XLVIII (1933).

[1] *Inventaire sommaire du fonds de l'amirauté de Dieppe*, by J. Darsel, typed.
[2] These documents had been used by S. Berbain: *Le comptoir français de Iuda (Ouidah) au XVIIIe siècle; Mémorandum de l'Institut français d'Afrique noire*, No. 3. Paris, 1942.

Vol. I. no. 1748 (collection Montbret 463). Dissertation on rivers, *inter alia*, **2714** of West Africa, eighteenth century.

no. 2428 (collection Montbret 693). Report and plan for the development **2715** of West African trade by Lagrange de Chécieux, eighteenth century.

no. 2431 (collection Montbret 479). Report by Pruneau de Pommegorge **2716** on the trade of Senegal, French Guinea and the rivers of Benin, 1752.

no. 2436. (collection Montbret 125). Description of a voyage made by **2717** Goupy to the West African coast and the West Indies, with maps, 1681. *Second supplement*

no. 1265 (collection Montbret 867). Report on Senegal and the island of **2718** Goree, and information about the slave trade, 1754.

St. Brieuc

Town Library

Bibliothèque municipale de Saint-Brieuc, Côtes-du-Nord

The reading room is open from Tuesday to Saturday from 10 a.m. to 12, and from 2 to 7 p.m., except from July 1 to 8.
Catalogue général des manuscrits des bibliothèques publiques de France, vol. XIII, Paris, 1891.

84. Collection including, *inter alia*, report on French trade with America **2719** and Guinea, 1750.

St. Omer

Town Library

Bibliothèque municipale, rue Saint-Bertin, St.-Omer

Catalogue général des manuscrits des bibliothèques publiques de France, vol. XLIII, Paris, 1904.

1037. Collection of letters written to the shipowner B. Tresca, by Captain **2720** Vaustabel and the trading company Mesmer of Cap Français, 1783.[1]

---

[1] These letters have been extensively used by G. Coolen, 'Négriers dunkerquois', in the *Bull. Soc. acad. des antiquaires de la Morinie*, xix, 1960.

Strasbourg

NATIONAL AND UNIVERSITY LIBRARY

Bibliothèque nationale et universitaire, 6 place de la république, Strasbourg

The reading room is open every day except Sunday from 9 a.m. to 10 p.m. There is a collection of maps, including some of West Africa, which is being reorganized.

Tours

TOWN LIBRARY

Bibliothèque municipale, place Anatole-France, Tours, Indre-et-Loire

Catalogue général des manuscrits des bibliothèques publiques de France, vol. XXXVII, Paris, 1900.

1139. Collection of documents, including some on the Guinea trade, destroyed in 1910.   **2721**

Vannes

DEPARTMENTAL ARCHIVES

Archives départementales du Morbihan, 2 rue Alain-Le-Grand, Vannes

The reading room is open from Monday to Friday from 9 a.m. to 12, and from 2 to 6 p.m., and on Saturdays from 9 a.m. to 12, except from July 1 to 15. The archives of the Admiralty of Vannes and of the naval port of Lorient are conserved in Vannes, and there is a *Répertoire numérique de la Série B, 8–14 B,* by P. Thomas-Lacroix, Vannes, 1943, which covers these two series as well as the archives of the consulate of Vannes and Lorient, and includes an alphabetical list of the ships involved.

Series 9 B. *Amirauté de Vannes*[1]

The most promising groups of documents for information about West **2722**
Africa are *9 B 30–55*, minutes, 1716–1807 (incomplete).

E.g. *54*. Declarations of negro slaves imported into France and certifi-
cates of liberation, 1736–77. *65–76*. Commissions of ships, 1704–79
(incomplete). *77–83*. Reports by captains, 1692–1784.

96–9. Log-books.   **2723**

E.g. *99*. Part of log of the *Saint-Louis* during voyage to Senegal,
1729–31.

[1] See introductory note to section of the Archives of the Ministry of Marine, p. 89.

INDEX

Transliterations of African place-names and personal names vary greatly in spelling, e.g. 'Ouerre and 'Owerri'. The more common form is given, with cross-references where identification is possible. The names of ships are set in italics.

INDEX

159

Casamance, 1149, 1246, 1272–3, 1281, 1287, 1595, 1726, 1753, 1779, 1834, 2057, 2514, 2706
Casaunau, 237, 253, 260. *Cf.* Cazaneau *below*
Cassini river, 1813
Castaigne, J., notary of Bordeaux, 2528
Castellan, captain, 1039
Castelnaux, captain, 952, 954
Castor, 841, 855
Castries, Charles-Eugène-Gabriel, marquess de, 2514, 2519, 2590
Castries, 1061
Catalonia, 2621
Cauchoise, 1079
Caumont, captain de, 1053
Cayenne, 714
Cayor, 1748, 1774–6, 1802–4; lake, 2535
Cazalis, captain, 2622
Cazaneau, captain, 873. *Cf.* Casaunau *above*
Cazejus, captain, 2623
Cérès, 1009–10
César, 1005
Chad, 1486, 1506, 1573, 2009
Chambonneau, 76
Chameau, 800
Champeau, King, 2679
Champenoise, 1089
Chapelet, missionary, 631
Charente, 857, 1075
Chari, 1506, 1988
Charlemagne, 2630
Charpentier, 171, 210, 302, 2057
Chasseur, captain, 994
Chastelus, de, 1713
Chaurand frères, 2648–51
Chécieux, Lagrange de, 2715
Cherbe river, 2148
Chevalier, missionary, 631
Chevalier Marin, 990–1
Cheval-Marin, 424
Chevigny, de, 790
Chevreau, 637
China, 2539
Cholet, 1483
Choquet, 244
Chouquet, captain, 881, 947
Cigale, 452
Cigogne, 811
Clergeau, 1426
Clion, 153, 256, 259
Coeuvres, Berthrand de, 2677
Colbert, Jean-Baptiste, 2092
Colin, G., 1725–6
Colin and Co., 1277
Collé, commander of Galam, 2057
Colombier, captain, 1040–1

Colombin of Nantes, 2057
Comète, 859
Compagnie d'Afrique, 15, 57, 650, 1226
Compagnie d'Angole, 589
Compagnie d'Asient, 651, 728, 730, 2666
Compagnie de Galam et Dualo, 1903
Compagnie de Guinée, 652, 1201, 2081
Compagnie de Guyane, 2659, 2667
Compagnie de Sénégal, 54–633 *et passim*
Compagnie des Indes occidentales, 18, 141, 149–50, 156, 654, 1199, 1224, 1226, 1953, 2057, 2542, 2666, 2673, 2675
Compagnie d'Occident, 652
Compagnie royale d'Afrique, 1224, 2068
Compagnon, map by, 2398
Company of Emden, 663
Company of Ostend, 2079
Comte d'Artois, 2530
Comte de Forcalquier, 2586
Comte de Jarnac, 2588
Comtesse, 401–2, 886, 890, 897–8, 979
Conference of Paris, 1258
Congo, 1100, 1259, 1260, 1275, 1501, 1591, 1966, 2002, 2009, 2624
Congo and Gabon, map of, 2604
Congo, Independent State of, 1520
Congo river, 1503, 2531
Constant, captain, 298
Constantine, 1225
Content, 1045
Copaux, captain, 919
Corbie, G., captain, 2566
Corisco, bay, 1169
Corrette, 240, 266
Cosroë, 1282, 1967
Côte Malaguette, 1193
Cotonou, 2005
Coulombe, captain de, 902
Courchamp, Philippe Hanion de, captain, 2647
Couridoux, 1422
Courrier d'Orléans, 942, 950–1, 955–6, 976
Courserac, captain, 1015
Courtois, map by, 2016–23
Cousine, 1066
Crasson, captain, 1020–1
Crassous de Médeuil, J., captain, 2567
Creney, captain de, 903
Creoles, 1474
Croiseur, 842
Crozet, captain, 570
Cumba, Antonio-José dà, 2703
Cussy, de, 2056
Cuverville, de, 1475
Cybèle, 995, 998
Cygne, 989